And others, Arthur Cleveland

**The Genesis of the American Prayer Book**

A Survey of the Origin and Development of the Liturgy of the Church in the United States

And others, Arthur Cleveland

**The Genesis of the American Prayer Book**
*A Survey of the Origin and Development of the Liturgy of the Church in the United States*

ISBN/EAN: 9783337260248

Printed in Europe, USA, Canada, Australia, Japan

Cover: Foto ©Lupo / pixelio.de

More available books at **www.hansebooks.com**

# The Genesis of the American Prayer Book

### A Survey of the Origin and Development of the Liturgy of the Church in the United States

BY

Rt. Rev. A. Cleveland Coxe, D.D., LL.D.
Bishop of Western New York

Rt. Rev. George F. Seymour, D.D., LL.D.
Bishop of Springfield

Rt. Rev. William Stevens Perry, D.D., LL.D., D.C.L.
Bishop of Iowa

and

Rt. Rev. William Croswell Doane, D.D., LL.D.
Bishop of Albany

### With an Appendix
on Changes Incorporated into the Prayer Book
BY THE
Rev. Samuel Hart, D.D.

### Edited with an Introduction
BY THE
Rev. C. Ellis Stevens, LL.D., D.C.L.

New York
JAMES POTT & CO., PUBLISHERS
1893

COPYRIGHT, 1892,
BY C. ELLIS STEVENS.

Press of J. J. Little & Co.
Astor Place, New York

TO

John Williams, D.D., LL.D.,

WHO AS
PRIMATE OF THE CHURCH IN THE UNITED STATES,
AND AS A LEADER IN THE
ESTABLISHMENT OF A
STANDARD PRAYER BOOK,
HAS PROVED HIMSELF SO WORTHY A
SUCCESSOR OF THE VENERATED

Bishop White,

THIS VOLUME—
WHICH GOES FORTH FROM THE HISTORIC FANE
WHERE THE AMERICAN PRAYER BOOK
WAS FIRST ADOPTED AND WHERE
RESTS THE SACRED DUST
OF THE
FATHER OF THE AMERICAN CHURCH—
IS
AFFECTIONATELY INSCRIBED.

# CONTENTS.

**Primitive Liturgies.**

By the Rt. Rev. A. CLEVELAND COXE, D.D., LL.D., Bishop of Western New York.

**The Reformation Prayer Books.**

By the Rt. Rev. GEORGE F. SEYMOUR, D.D., LL.D., Bishop of Springfield.

**Early American Prayer Books.**

By the Rt. Rev. WILLIAM STEVENS PERRY, D.D., LL.D., D.C.L., Bishop of Iowa, and Historiographer of the Church.

**The Prayer Book Enriched.**

By the Rt. Rev. WILLIAM CROSWELL DOANE, D.D., LL.D., Bishop of Albany, and Chairman of the Joint Committee of the General Convention on Liturgical Revision.

**Changes Incorporated into the Standard Prayer Book of 1892.**

By the Rev. SAMUEL HART, D.D., Professor in Trinity College, Hartford, Custodian of the Standard Prayer Book, Secretary of the House of Bishops, Secretary of the Joint Committee of the General Convention on Liturgical Revision, etc.

# INTRODUCTION.

The American Book of Common Prayer is historically associated with one sacred spot. The venerable fane of Christ Church, Philadelphia, is, in a special sense, its birthplace. And on that spot the American Church itself—as an independent national body owing no allegiance, save of love, to the Mother Church of England—came into organic being.

It was there that the first effort toward liturgical revision was made, at the first of the General Conventions of the Church—a Convention presided over by the then rector, William White. Dr. White had been a moving spirit in the measures leading up to this memorable council, and himself had formulated the principles on which the Church sought and attained organism. He and Dr. William Smith—also intimately associated with Christ Church—were chief promoters of the work of revision; and after the Convention they were left to complete and issue the "Proposed Book."

It was on that spot that the second General Convention met in 1786, and the third in 1789.

The last, which opened its sessions under the presidency of Bishop White, and later organized into a House of Bishops and a House of Deputies,[1] completed the Constitution of the Church, and formally set forth the American Prayer Book. At that altar the Holy Eucharist was celebrated by Dr. Smith, according to the form in the first Book of Edward VI., as adapted in the Scottish Use—the adoption of our present Communion Office immediately following the celebration. Before the same altar now rests the sacred dust of the Patriarch of the American Church.

It was there in 1883, that the opening session was held of that General Convention which began the work of the new liturgical revision and enrichment, now ended by the adoption of the Standard Prayer Book of 1892. And as the beginning of this latest revision was marked by services in the ancient church, so the completion of the revision was also marked. For during October, 1892, while the General Convention was in session in Baltimore putting final touches to the new Prayer Book, Bishops of the Church, held in reputation for liturgical scholar-

---

[1] The Secretary of the House of Deputies—the celebrated Francis Hopkinson, a vestryman of Christ Church—had been Secretary of Continental Congress.

ship and counting among them those officially connected with the revision work, went from the Convention, Sunday after Sunday, to Christ Church, Philadelphia, and delivered an historical course of sermons intended to go forth in published form, as, in some sort, a popular introduction to the new Book.[1]

Reference to such facts as these—facts sufficiently familiar to most Churchmen—may not be altogether amiss, as furnishing an explanation of the present volume, and adding point to its pages. Rather naturally, the course of sermons was retrospective. For scarcely a more fitting introduction of the new Prayer Book could be given, than that supplied by a study of origins. And the treatment of the theme thus selected has not been limited to American, or even English sources, but widens into the liturgic past of the Christian Ages, and stretches on and back, even to the day of Apostles and Prophets.

The volume now given to the public is not merely one of published preaching, but has been carefully adapted for general readers—so

---

[1] In this course, Bishop Doane, of Albany, as chairman of the committee on revision, gave the first general public announcement of the results of the liturgic action of the Convention.

that it goes freshly forth. From the olden sanctuary living forces reach out into the time, from memories of events that live in the life of the American Church forever.

There has been hope that widely differing minds might find these pages that follow, helpful. Not merely among ourselves who claim the Prayer Book, but among other many is the Prayer Book loved. And there are those of every Christian name, who, in this, are one with us at heart, and more and more becoming so in practice. Nor is such fact wholly strange. For all who count themselves of English blood, have in that blood a bond to bind them to the Prayer Book used by all their English forefathers before the days of sad division. Others in our land, who, though not of English blood, yet speak the old English tongue, have common heritage in sacred forms which mark its holiest utterance. And as the forms themselves are not merely English, but of the saintly past of the Church of all the saints, surely there is hope here for possible unities of the future, for which God may be even now preparing. In these days, at any rate, a widening interest is felt, and very keenly felt, in whatsoever has to do with liturgic worship, and with the Book of Common Prayer. And no word that one may honestly speak, even though with an earnestness running counter to another's convictions, will go unheeded. The Prayer Book of the Anglo-Saxon race is not for naught.

C. ELLIS STEVENS.

CHRIST CHURCH, Philadelphia,
    Advent, 1892.

# PRIMITIVE LITURGIES.

# PRIMITIVE LITURGIES.

THE old Prayer Book of our fathers now appears in a new edition. After a hundred years of loving usage by them and their children, and of steady gain on the affections of the American people, it has been subjected to revision, and has been made—not a new book, but, on the contrary—an older book than we have had before. The only important changes are restorations. We receive, anew, some precious features of ancient worship, which were omitted by our early revisers for reasons serious in their day but long since obsolete. The Church demands again, what was then reluctantly sacrificed to external objections that exist no more.

Even where they were, perhaps, mistaken, I reverence the revisers of 1792. Think what difficulties they encountered, in days which tried their spirits. The whole country was impoverished. Travelling was so expensive, and so tedious, as to forbid frequent gatherings for conference. Even correspondence was subject to a heavy tax and to long delays in transit to and fro—especially the needful correspondence with the Bishops of the Mother Church, and with the learned in Oxford and Cambridge. Libraries were scantily supplied, and liturgical works of merit were very rare, and could only be imported at great cost. All things considered, I must regard the result of their labours with astonishment, and as evidence that the Holy Spirit was with them, and answered their prayers.

When it was resolved to submit their work to a fresh revision, fears were entertained, even by supporters of this movement, lest the endeared devotions of our childhood should be superseded by something new and strange. But, after all that has been said and done; after the suggestions and discussions of long years and of many local and some general councils—what a eulogy upon the past is the outcome. Very little has been altered, after all. With the more important changes we are already familiarized by authorized use. Our services will go on, with no shock upon our sense of continuity and identity. Even the "flexibility" that has been conceded, under the pressure of missionary experience and because of services greatly multiplied, is not designed to change the order of the Morning and Evening Prayer, except where it is necessary or entirely acceptable to the people. It is limited by *discretion*, not abandoned to caprice: and in all cases, is subject to the godly judgment and counsels of the Ordinary.[1]

---

[1] The following extract is from the sermon as originally delivered in Christ Church, Philadelphia: "It was a happy thought of your rector to institute a course of lectures introductory to the new Prayer Book. He wisely judged, that, here and now, such a course might, for obvious reasons, be made serviceable to the whole Church. *Now*—because a period of liturgic study and of the practical adoption of our Book by the most devout and intelligent Christians of our country is recognized as near. And *here*—because with these hallowed walls of Christ Church, Philadelphia, the history of the Prayer Book is identified. Here we are worshipping, to-day, close by the reverend relics of your illustrious rector, the apostolic White; with whose life and labours, every page of the Prayer Book is so intimately associated. As one of the few survivors who remember his person and his ministrations, I deeply feel the privilege of standing in this pulpit, where, for more than half a century, he proclaimed the blessed Gospel so faithfully and so well. And may I venture to say, that this same pulpit is tenderly endeared to me, by the reflection that here, in old Colonial days, has stood an ancestor of my own, whose bones repose in your own cemetery. He died the missionary rector of New Castle, Delaware; in some degree a martyr to his zeal for the Prayer Book, and one of the founders of our national Church.

"Yes, this is the sacred spot where the revised edition of this memorable year may be appropriately introduced to the nation. For here, the Father of his

The grateful task assigned to me, is introductory to what will follow from able bishops in the course of this book. It is my duty to speak of the primitive liturgies of the Christian Church, out of which the Prayer Book is compiled. In the *first* place, let me direct your attention to a Scriptural view of the genesis of liturgic worship; and so prepare you, in the *second* place, for what I must say of early Christian worship, and of those treasures of ages which it has bequeathed to us, in the Book of Common Prayer.

I. For the elements of our liturgical system, we must go back to the earliest years of human history. We are told that by the faith and sacrifice of Abel, " he, being dead, yet speaketh." Of what does he speak ? Of nothing less than the Creed of all the faithful—of the Atoning Sacrifice of the Lamb of God, to which all the typical sacrifices of the Patriarchal and the Mosaic worshippers pointed before the Incarnation; to which the sacrificial commemorations

---

Country was among the first of those who welcomed the American Liturgy. Imagine his emotions, when he, who had been educated to pray for King George and the High Court of Parliament, heard the fervent responses of his fellow-worshippers praying for him as their President, and for the Senate and Representatives of the young Republic in Congress assembled."

of Christian worship point backward in like manner; to which the liturgy of Heaven, now and evermore, bears witness in the perpetual anthem of the redeemed: "Worthy is the Lamb that was slain."

Sacrificial worship, inspired by faith in Christ, is the only worship that God accepts. Cain, the original of all unbelief, rejected such worship; and he with his empty tribute was rejected as well. But, here, we must not forget that the sacrifice of Calvary was the one offering, for the sins of the whole world, which alone is propitiatory. Once offered, it was anticipated beforehand and it is commemorated until now; but it cannot be repeated; though, thank God, it is applied to our souls in the sacraments. To this great principle all Scripture bears witness; more especially the Epistle to the Hebrews, which expounds the liturgic system, as it existed before the Incarnation, and as it was instituted by the blessed Apostles in the nobler worship of the Christian Church.

And this brings me to St. Paul's remarkable expression in the following text: "I have written somewhat boldly to you, my brethren, that I might put you afresh in remembrance, concerning the grace which is given to me of God; that I should be a *Liturge* of Jesus Christ among the Gentiles,[1] *ministering as a priest,* the gospel of God; that the oblation of the Gentiles might be acceptable, being sanctified by the Holy Ghost." In this close rendering of the original I have been forced to deprive it of the beauty of our Version, in order to direct your attention to the following facts: (1.) That the Apostle here adopts liturgical words and ideas, in harmony with the sacrificial teaching of the Epistle to the Hebrews, throwing great light upon that Epistle. Not less does it harmonize with the Epistle from which I have quoted it, and to which, as he declares, it supplied a key. (2.) That he thus asserts his priesthood and the sacrificial character of the Christian worship. (3.) That he does this, glorying in the grandeur of the Catholic priesthood, among all nations, as contrasted with the isolated and effete and purely typical priesthood of the Law. (4) That his language, here, expounds the text from Malachi, with which our Daily Service so properly begins, when it immediately precedes the Eucharist; and (5) that it lends illustration to the words of our blessed Master himself, at the well of Samaria: "Woman, believe me, the hour cometh, when neither in this mountain nor in

---

[1] Rom. xv. 16.

Jerusalem shall ye worship the Father"—that is to say, exclusively. For, when it comes to the oblation of the Gentiles, a Catholic worship is promised, according to Malachi: [1] "From the rising of the sun, even unto the going down of the same, my name shall be great among the Gentiles, and in every place incense shall be offered unto my name, and a pure *oblation of bread and wine;* for my name shall be great among the Gentiles, saith the Lord of hosts."

For a view of this Apostolic system of worship let me recall the first pages of your Prayer Book. Have you ever reflected upon the significance of those tables which meet your eyes as you open it? They are (1) the Tables for the Daily Prayers and Lessons, with the Psalter, for the weeks and months of every year, and then (2) the "Tables to find Easter," pointing to the great Paschal system of the Church; the Eucharistic worship and great festive Communion of Easter, with those of every Lord's day or weekly Easter, and of all the satellite feasts that surround the Easter sunshine. Grasp, therefore, with respect to public worship, these two great ideas of the Prayer Book and of the Holy Scriptures: (1) The perpetual Scriptural ministering of the

---

[1] Mal. i. 11.

Gospel which Malachi predicts, and concerning which St. Paul asserts his own priesthood, just as elsewhere he speaks of the Christian altar;[1] and (2) the auxiliary and dependent Common Prayer to which all the faithful are entitled daily wherever two or three may meet together in the Master's name.

But to learn how ancient is this divine plan of worship let us take another step, and advance from the fundamental truth inscribed on Abel's altar to that which was revealed to the Father of the faithful, and which was made more and more explicit, age after age, as the great epoch of the Gospel was drawing nigh. In the Book of Genesis we read of Melchizedek, and for the first time we meet the word "priest." This mysterious personage comes before Abraham as "the priest of the Most High God;" not *a* priest, but *the* priest. St. Paul declares that his is the only priesthood. It had its types in the Law and has its ministerial representatives in the New Covenant. He only abides forever, the "Priest upon His throne." His commissioned servants, ministering in His Name, represent His priesthood to all believers and apply its benefits to their fellow-men. All Christians, in their divers relations, are [2] "a holy and a

---

[1] Heb. viii. 10.   [2] I. Pet. ii. 5–9.

royal priesthood to offer up spiritual sacrifices acceptable to God by Jesus Christ." But over all, He is "the Great *High Priest*," the true Melchizedek[1] who, "when he had offered one sacrifice for sins forever, sat down on the right hand of God."

Now, St. Paul argues that this apparition was vouchsafed to Abraham, not only to give the Father of all believers clearer ideas of the promised Messiah than had been vouchsafed before, but to put upon everlasting record His true Priesthood; in order that the Mosaic priesthood might understand their position as bare types, a foreshadowing symbol for a transient period, interposed till He should come who should put them away forever. This He was to do by offering Himself as the true Paschal Lamb, and then establishing a better priesthood to commemorate His sacrifice on earth, while He presents it in heaven. Thus, then, the bloody sacrifices of the Law being put away, what takes their place? St. Paul tells us, as Malachi had predicted it. It was the oblation which Melchizedek showed to Abraham when "he brought forth bread and wine." St. Paul, therefore, abrogates the Levitical priesthood, and asserts the superior antiquity

---

[1] Heb. x. 12.

of that which was thus foreshown four hundred years before Moses established his typical priests. Our Lord Himself says: "Your father Abraham rejoiced to see my day: and he saw it, and was glad."

Thus I have shown that the Liturgy of the Gospel was asserted and provided for nearly two thousand years before the Incarnation, and that the Christian Eucharist was "the sacrificial ministering of the Gospel" which St. Paul claimed; something he might boast of as better than the priesthood which the Eternal Priest abolished forever when He said, "It is finished." He had seen Melchizedek.

Reflect that by a provision of the Law it was foreordained that when this which is perfect should come, then that which was incomplete should be done away.[1] It was commanded that the sacrifices of the Law should be offered *only in Jerusalem*. So then, when the Temple was destroyed in that very generation, there remained only the divine system of the New Covenant. Out of the Law had appeared, in consummate beauty, the whole system which it presignified. It, therefore, was decayed,[2] and "waxing old, was ready to vanish away."

---

[1] Compare Heb. vii. 19, and I. Cor. xiii. 10.
[2] Heb. viii. 13.

And now turn to the divine provision for the daily office of prayer and praise with reading of the Scriptures, which are the auxiliary services preparatory for the right use of the Holy Eucharist. For the origin of these, one must go back to the "Institutions of Samuel," a thousand years before the Advent.[1] This prophet, who was himself a very striking type of Christ, stands forth as the founder of a new and more evangelical series of those holy prophets, "which have been since the world began." We find him founding "schools of the prophets," and instituting a new order of public worship, dependent upon the service of the Temple, but bringing home to every Israelite in the villages of Palestine opportunities of evangelical devotion, and of hearing the Law and the Prophets "read in course, with prayer." At the Passover and other festivals they went up to the Temple for sacrifice. In the synagogues they enjoyed the offices of prayer and psalmody, and the hearing of the Scriptures, at least every Sabbath day.

It was after Samuel's time that synagogues were multiplied, adorned with carved work, and with goodly cedars. To provide for the edification of the people,[2] in these "houses of

---
[1] Compare I. Sam. x. 5, 10, 11, and xix. 24.
[2] Ps. lxxiv. 6–9.

prayer," we find Samuel establishing what we now call divinity schools. In these colleges they were instructed in sacred music and the chanting of such hymns as those of Moses and Miriam, or those of Deborah and Hannah. Thus we read of the "hill of God,"[1] where a company of prophets met Saul "coming down from the high place with a psaltery" and other instruments, and prophesying, apparently by divine inspiration. Here it may be well to note the earliest reference to the *Psaltery*, from which the name of the *Psalter* comes into our devotions. Again,[2] after many years, we read: "Saul sent messengers to take David: and when they saw the company of the prophets prophesying, and Samuel standing *as appointed* over them, the spirit of God was upon the messengers of Saul." Here Samuel appears as a leader, overseer or bishop among the prophets, presiding over their solemnities; and this was at Naioth, which, the learned tell us, was a collection of dwellings for the schools, such as continued to the times of Elisha; although under Solomon's son, Rehoboam, we read of the invaders from Egypt, that "they burnt up all the houses of God in the land."[3] The

---

[1] I. Sam. x. 5.  [2] I. Sam. xix. 20.
[3] Ps. lxxiv. 9.

synagogue worship had, therefore, been largely established, and in these synagogues, as in the Temple also, the Psalter was the very life of the public worship of the Most High. For now we come to the great act of Samuel's life and mission. He anointed David not only to be king, in the room of Saul, but also to be "the sweet psalmist of Israel."[1] "The spirit of the Lord came upon David from that day forward."[2] In brief, the Psalter was created by his inspired genius. It vertebrates the entire worship of the Church of this day. And so our Common Prayer comes to us from the prophet Samuel. Thus we derive that miracle of devotional poetry, which for nearly three thousand years has been dear to all believers, in all lands; which was sung in the synagogues of the Hebrews, and more majestically chanted by the singers of the Temple in their courses; which the daughters of Jerusalem could not sing in a strange land, when they sat down by the rivers of Babylon and wept to remember Zion; which our Divine Lord so often referred to and quoted, as did His Apostles afterwards; which the Holy Church throughout all the world, in divers tongues, has used perpetually since their day; which has consoled the saints in the times

---

[1] II. Sam. xxiii. 1.   [2] I. Sam. xvi. 13.

of persecution, and which they have sung at the stake, amid flames of fire; which has refreshed millions of the faithful upon their death-beds, and which has made part of the offices of their burial. These are the psalms which the early Christians intoned as they pushed the plowshare through the furrows, or with which they solaced their daily toil at the anvil or the loom. The maiden sung the Psalter as she twirled the thread of her distaff; and not less, holy men rose at midnight to sing psalms, as it were, with Paul and Silas in the stocks. And, in our own time, how many among us who have grown old and have recited the Psalter, month after month, from the days of youth, can bear witness to the marvellous adaptation of its oracles to the changing conditions of life; to prosperity and tribulation, to joy and sorrow, to health and to infirmity, to moments of rapture and to moments which but for its comfortable words would darken to despair. It is true, there are words in the Psalter which remind us of God's retributive dealings with those who rejected the Messiah; but they may be profitably used by all who would not become "as a man that heareth not, and in whose mouth are no reproofs."[1] With words from the

---

[1] Ps. xxxviii. 14.

Psalter our Divine Lord prayed to the Father on the cross; with like words He resigned His spirit as He gave up the ghost; and, quoting the same Psalm which foretold His death, He first saluted His disciples as His "brethren" when He rose from the dead. This same Psalter lends its imagery to the words of Jesus: "I am the Good Shepherd;" and again to the language of the Apocalypse: "He shall feed them, and shall lead them unto living fountains of waters." There seems to be a reference to the title of the greatest of the Paschal Psalms, and to its entire prediction of the Atonement and Redemption, when our Lord, among His last words to the Church, exclaimed: "I am the root and the offspring of David, and the bright morning star."

II. Such, by pre-arrangement and gradual introduction, was the divine plan of love and mercy for supplying the infant Church with systematic forms of worship, from the moment of Christ's ascending to His throne and sending forth His Vicar Spirit to abide with her forever. The synagogue worship—restored under Ezra, and supplied with the Psalter, the Law and the Prophets—was also enriched with other prayers and devotions. Much is implied in the fact, that John had taught his disciples how to pray in accordance with the new revelations of his mission. His requirements of acts of penitence and faith and the public confession of sins, as qualifications for his baptism, suggest this inference. And when the disciples asked the Lord for further instructions, we may believe that, with His incomparable prayer, He gave them many other teachings, which the Spirit afterward brought to their remembrance. His own sublime summary of devotion seems to be referred to as the very corner-stone of this fabric of Common Prayer, when the Apostle speaks of the Spirit, "whereby we cry *Abba*, Father."[1] The responsive *Amen* is familiarly mentioned as following Eucharistic praise.[2] A French author[3] very suggestively imagines that the prophetic gifts which St. Paul endeavours to subordinate to uses of public worship, made the common prayers of the primitive believers an "office of the Holy Ghost;" and to this our own Matins and Evensong correspond, in the abundant use which they include of the words of Inspiration; "the lively oracles" of God. When, after the day of Pentecost, Christian doxologies were added, by the inspired gifts imparted so freely, even to laymen and godly women; when the

---

[1] Rom. viii. 15–17. [2] I. Cor. xiv. 16.
[3] Origines du Culte, par L'Abbé Duchesne, Paris, 1889.

Evangelical Hymns, preserved by St. Luke, were brought into use ; when "forms of sound words" became familiar—including, we may safely suppose, what we now call the Creeds, at least in their elemental forms—it wanted only what came so soon, the writings of the Evangelists and Apostles, to supply the Common Prayer of Christians in all the fullness requisite to their constant assemblings. "With one accord" they lifted up their voices in their congregations. And, as the Apostles immediately took order for the great central act of worship, we see that everything which we regard as necessary to Divine Service came into existence, out of the elements of the Law—even as our Lord Himself came forth from the sepulchre in His Resurrection from the Dead.

It is written, therefore, of the Apostolic Church at the very beginning: "They continued stedfastly in the Apostles' doctrine and fellowship, in the breaking of Bread, and in the Prayers."[1] Observe the significance of these four particulars. The Prayers, the Eucharistic Oblation, the Apostolic fellowship, and the Apostolic Creed, are recognized as something definite, organized, understood, received and steadily maintained by all. Here is essentially

---

[1] Acts ii. 42.

the Prayer Book in its original. The matured system is referred to, not infrequently, by St. Paul, who "ordained" one system "in all the churches."[1] He praises those who "held fast the *traditions*," as he delivered them;[2] he commends a like stedfastness with respect to the "form of sound words," which Timothy had heard from the Apostle himself;[3] and he says to the Thessalonians: "We command you in the name of our Lord Jesus Christ, that ye withdraw yourselves from every brother that walketh disorderly, and not after the tradition which he received of us."[4] Even what we now call "the rubrical system" is here implied, and seems more especially recognized in the words, "Let all things be done decorously and *in order:*"[5] where this word *order* is the Greek *taxis*—of which the root idea is familiarized among us in the word *tactics*, whereby artificial arrangement, or prescribed method, is universally understood.

It agrees with all that seems here implied, when we not only find evidence, that the Apostolic ordinances were delivered with unity of plan throughout the whole Church from India to Britain, even before the death of St. John;

---

[1] I. Cor. vii. 17.  [2] Or "ordinances," I. Cor. vii. 2.
[3] II. Tim. 1-13.  [4] II. Thess. iii. 6.
[5] I. Cor. xiv. 40.

but that the Liturgies which have come down to us from remote antiquity, are marked by uniformity and variety, in proportions nearly equal. And here we use the word *Liturge* in its strict sense, as the name of the Eucharistic Service; to which St. Paul seems to point, when he couples his claim to be a *Liturgy* with the assertion of his Hierurgic, or priestly ministration. The ancient Liturgies bear the name of Churches founded by the Apostles; or of the Apostles themselves who are supposed to have founded them. And it is to be noted that they all originated in the East, even the Liturgy of Rome bearing marks of Greek authorship. We must keep in mind, however, that we have no very ancient manuscripts of these Liturgies—a fact for which it is not difficult to account. Yet we can trace their essential features to a very early date; and nothing but a primitive antiquity can account for their harmonies, or even for their diversities. It would otherwise be hard to explain the truth, that they are all reducible to *three families* of ritual, classified by their family features and birth-marks. (1) We have the great Oriental family, bearing the names respectively of St. James of Jerusalem, St. Mark, St. Paul and St. Chrysostom. The two last named are so nearly the same as to be practically one, and they are in use at this day in Russia and elsewhere—disfigured, it is true, by interpolations. To them may be added the Liturgy of Eastern Syria. But superlatively beautiful, scriptural and rich in devotional expression is the Liturgy of St. James. Its incrustations and corruptions are comparatively slight, and may be easily detected by comparison with ancient writings. (2) The Gallican family is derived from Ephesus, and is supposed to represent the tradition of St. John. The originals were undoubtedly brought to Lyons by Pothinus; of whom we know something from the writings of Irenæus, his successor in the bishopric. With this family, the early Liturgies of Britain were near of kin; for the Churches of the Britons and the Gauls were closely allied from the beginning and were practically one down to the time when the Saxons invaded the British isle. (3) The Roman rite, which was singularly devoid of Oriental warmth, included, nevertheless, the essential characteristics of its parentage. And, as improved by the Patriarch Gregory, in the sixth century, it became, in time, predominant in the West; though not entirely so in France and Spain, and never in England.

It must not be forgotten, that the ancient Church of Britain was planted by the disciples of St. Paul, who himself had preached to Britons while they were captives in Rome. And this Church is the first that appears in history in the form of nationalized Christianity. Separated, by its insularity, from frequent contact with Southern Europe, it was forgotten in the Roman capital, and Gregory heard of its existence with surprise. His missionary, Augustine, asked him what he should do with those original Christians of Britain whose liturgic system differed, in so many particulars, from his own. Gregory was not a pope, for he abhorred the very thought of a Universal Bishop, as anti-Christian; and his answer is in entire harmony with his character. He instructed Augustine in the following words: " You were bred in the Roman Church and know its custom. . . . But if you have found anything in the Gallican, or any other Church, more acceptable to God, carefully make choice of the same and teach the (Saxon) Church of the English, which is new in the Faith, whatsoever you may gather from the several Churches. For things are not to be loved for the sake of places, but places for the sake of good things."[1]

---

[1] The Abbé Duchesne (p. 94, *ut supra*) is so amazed at these instructions, that he thinks they must be a forgery, "because *no pope* could have written such

Now, the Liturgy of these primitive Britons was full of the Oriental features which came to them from Ephesus. And it must be borne in mind, that, with some differences that had been gradually introduced, its rites and usages were observed from Cornwall and Wales, northward to Northumberland and even to Scotland, and westward to Ireland. It is now common to speak of this wide-spread communion as "the Celtic Church," and of its rites and usages as those of the "Celtic Liturgy." It is thus described by a learned writer of our own day:[1] "The facts present to our view a vast Celtic communion . . . sending its missions among Teutonic tribes on the Continent and to distant isles like Iceland; Catholic in doctrine and practice . . . with a long roll of saints, every name and note of which is either that of one like St. Columbanus *taking a line wholly independent of Rome,* or like Bishop Colman, *directly in collision with her;* having its own Liturgy, its own translation of the Bible, its own mode of chanting, its own monastic rule, its own cycle for the calculation of Easter, and

---

words." Very true; he was not a pope, and the words by which he rejected the "Universal Bishopric," are much less like a pope.

[1] Liturgy of the Celtic Church, by F. E. Warren, B. D., Oxford, 1871.

presenting both internal and external evidences of complete autonomy." It was on account of this autonomy, or national character, that Rome, as she herself declined from her Catholic character and created her schism with the Churches of the East, saw fit to "ignore or impugn" the superior claims of the Celtic Church to Catholicity: but this, because she forgot the maxims of Gregory, and the great Canon of Catholicity which permits diversity of usages—so long as everything is preserved which not only "everywhere and by all the Churches" has been accepted; but which they have accepted *always*, from the beginnings of Christianity.

The Roman Missal was improved by the Patriarch Gregory, and it came into England in a condition well-suited to the wants of the newly-converted Saxons. It was not a Mass Liturgy as that word is now understood—a liturgy, that is, in which the people have no share and are not bidden to Holy Communion. There was Communion in both kinds, and non-communicants were excluded. The heresy of transubstantiation had not been invented, and hence the host was not lifted up to be adored. Unfortunately, the Saxon dialect was regarded as barbarism; and as the missionaries of Gregory could only celebrate in the Latin tongue, this violation of the Scriptural injunction led to the unhappy departures from Scriptural truth which followed. The liturgical principle perishes when the priest takes it all to himself, and robs the laity of their ability and their privilege of responding an intelligent and fervent *Amen* to his " giving of thanks."

So then, there were in the British Isle, after Gregory's mission to the Saxons, two distinct Churches, with their respective Liturgies—the ancient British Church, which had been there from the Apostles' times, and the Church of the evangelized Saxons, who had driven the Britons out of the southern and southeastern coasts.

Gradually, under the pressure of circumstances, the people of Britain became fused into one nation and one Church. In a word, Britain became "England," and the stronger race of the Anglo-Saxons predominated. The Norman Conquest introduced the next great era in the history of our forefathers, and the greatest liturgical diversities.

For the Normans brought into England those debased and heretical ideas which had been propagated after the days of Charlemagne. The schism of Nicholas I. was the source of all these evils, and he must be regarded as the founder of the Papacy, as it was understood in Western Europe in those Mediæval Ages, which are justly denominated "Dark Ages." Even the most bigoted Ultramontane authors are forced to admit the awful wickedness which overwhelmed the See of Rome in the ninth and tenth centuries, when the Papacy had become established by means of the fraudulent Decretals, and, favoured by the almost universal ignorance of the times, was able to extend its abominations over "the Roman Empire" of Charles the Great. Of those popes who immediately succeeded Nicholas, even Moehler exclaims—"hell hath swallowed them up."[1] But hear the testimony of Génébrard, Archbishop of Aix, who used these words: *"During a hundred and fifty years about fifty popes have fallen away from the virtues of their predecessors, being apostates, or apostatical rather than apostolical."*[2] It was just when the Papal power had culminated in Hildebrand, who first commanded the name of "Pope" to be exclusively ascribed to the Roman bishop,[3] that the Normans broke into England and introduced mediæval doctrines and usages, wholly unscriptural and in conflict with the Catholic Councils.

---

[1] (A. D. 1537-97.)
[2] Littledale's Plain Reasons, p. 209.
[3] Anciently all bishops were called *papa*.

Hildebrand was all the more mischievous, because he was honest and in his way a reformer; but his errors arose from his supposition that the Decretals were genuine records, and his belief that by asserting their false claims in the most absolute way, he could improve the condition of things in the Latin Churches.

Never, for a moment, however, did the Church of England lose her identity by absorption with the established Church of the so-called "Holy Roman Empire," which Charlemagne had set up. She maintained that stubborn independence of spirit which the Celtic Church had imparted to her. By usurpation, persistently introduced, and not less persistently resisted, the pontiffs domineered, more or less, for five hundred years, over the Church of England; but their "supremacy" was never for a moment acknowledged, nor was it ever successfully enforced upon the Anglican or the Gallican Church. How few understand these facts or their immense significance!

These remarks are made necessary if we would comprehend, what I must next introduce, the subject of the variety of Liturgies that existed in England all through the period of the Papal ascendency. The Roman Liturgy was never admitted as the Liturgy of the Church of England. Turn to the Preface of the Book of

Common Prayer, when it first appeared in 1549, and we find in it these notable words: "Heretofore there hath been *great diversity* in saying and singing in churches within this realm, some following Salisbury use, some Hereford use, some the use of Bangor, some of York, and some of Lincoln; now, from henceforth all the whole realm *shall have but one use.*" Thus we owe to this blessed book, not only the creation of uniformity in Anglican worship, but its dissemination through all the world, among all English-speaking people, as a bond of unity, such as no other people in the world enjoy.

Of these various Uses, suffice it to say that "Salisbury Use" was in the ascendant down to the times of our restorers—they must not be confounded with mere "reformers"—who gathered out of it much wealth of material, but who, in so doing, were forced to remember the words of Scripture, "Thou shalt be as my mouth . . . if thou take forth the precious from the vile."

And most conspicuously were these two elements compounded in the "Use of Sarum"—for greatly was it enriched beyond the "Roman Use;" and yet even more did it embody the corruption and the novelties of the Hildebrandine era, as they multiplied through those dark times and changed the whole idea of the Catholic

Eucharist into that of the ceremonial Mass, at which nobody but the priest was a communicant, which took away the chalice from the people when they were permitted to receive at all, and which educated them to receive only once in the year. But, in all this, observe again, the overruling Providence of God. Had the barren Missal of Rome predominated, there would have been little of the precious to take forth from its poor material. It was less adulterated than the Sarum Use, but the latter was like ore that yields an enormous percentage of gold, when tried in the fire. That Use was introduced by Bishop Osmund, in less than twenty years after the Norman invasion; and it prevailed because of its "special beauties," in spite of the novelties of mediæval superstition, and the strange and anti-Catholic ceremonies whereby it gradually overlaid, and almost smothered, the Scriptural worship of the ancient Churches. Such were marketable Masses for souls in purgatory, which wholly deprived the sacrifice of the "pure oblation." Its terrible fault was its destructive operation on the great principle of Holy Communion, and its crime against the one sacrifice of the Cross, as the only propitiatory sacrifice for sin.

In bringing so great a subject to a conclusion,

we must not fail to note those important specialties of the Eastern Liturgies, the Oblation and Invocation, which, by the inestimable services of Bishop Seabury, were restored to our American Use, from the Scottish Liturgy of 1604; but not less from the first Anglican Prayer Book of the previous century. Without anticipating what others will more fully illustrate for your edification, in the chapters that are to follow, it is due to my own task to remind you that these ennobling usages come to us with the seal of an antiquity which mounts up to the age nearest to that of the Apostles. St. Cyril, of Jerusalem, regards them as originating in that Maternal See of the whole Church, in the days of St. James. That these features give special honour to the prophecy of Malachi which I have compared with the corresponding text from St. Paul, must be obvious; but that is a small matter compared with the tribute they pay to the whole spirit of Scripture, as it bears on the Atonement of Christ, His vicarious sacrifice, His everlasting priesthood, and His one oblation of Himself, once offered, to take away the sins of the world. No longer bleed the turtle-doves, or the young pigeons; no more the lambs of the Passover supply the typical blood of sprinkling. The Lamb of God is come, and has made all things new. Nor is it less important, possibly, to note that in the Invocation we glorify the Holy Spirit for His efficient work and His essential operation in the Sacraments. Let me, also, remind you of that feature of the Eucharist which raises into rapture the grand idea of the communion of saints, and which is found in all the Liturgies of Apostolic Christendom, from the beginning until now. I speak of the Prefaces and the *Tersanctus:* "Therefore with Angels and Archangels, and with all the company of heaven," etc. Of this many ritual writers have ventured to say, that it has never been unheard whenever, in a true Church, the Eucharist has been celebrated. On the great festivals of Christmas, Easter, and Pentecost, when I stand at the altar and recite these heavenly formulas, I seem, like the Apostle, to be caught up into Paradise, and to hear, among saints made perfect, "unspeakable words" which correspond with ours. Surely, it is something that must minister to the soul the most elevating and the purest emotions—the thought of those, the millions gone before us, "the great cloud of witnesses," whose lives and deaths have been uplifted to God by these same devotions, by anthems and alleluias that anticipate the joys of heaven. "Who is sufficient for these things?" Who is worthy to minister before the Lord in such a heaven brought down to earth? Blessed be He, who, unworthy as we are, "makes us able ministers of the New Covenant," by the gifts of His anointing, so that we offer "acceptable sacrifices" Godward; while manward we bear to our brethren the food of angels, and the cup of blessing which is filled from the heart of Jesus—from the water and the blood of His wounded side.

Welcome, then, anew, that Book of Common Prayer, made more precious than ever, which comes from the Council; from our apostles, presbyters, and brethren, convened under the Invocation of the Spirit, and remembered in the supplications of all our churches. Reflect when you devoutly unfold its pages, like the Bride in the Canticles, you open to the believer "that spring shut up, that fountain sealed." You offer the fragrance, also, of ardent love, the smell of "spikenard and all trees of frankincense and myrrh and all the chief spices;" you draw from the "fountain of gardens;" you drink from a "well of living waters and streams from Lebanon."

For the Prayer Book is not only a poem, or an oratorio from beginning to end, a choral-song, and a perpetual feast; it is not merely a well undefiled, of our mother-tongue, and, hardly excepting the English Bible, the first standard and classic of the language. To the anointed eye and ear it is infinitely more. Its "streams from Lebanon" are nothing less than the "fresh springs" that gush from Holy Writ, as from the Smitten Rock of Moses; from its Patriarchs and Prophets, its sweet singers, its Apostles and Evangelists. Those "gardens" and fountains of chaste delights, are, as you have been reminded, the litanies and hymns of all Saints; the Liturgies of the martyrs and confessors who have handed down to us the Holy Scriptures and the gifts that come by the Laying-on of hands.

Oh! infinite privilege of the devout worshipper, who, when he uses this Book, brings himself into spiritual communion with those faithful ones of old times, with every land and speech, with millions of his brethren praying with him, in all parts of the world. "Look upon the city of our solemnities; thine eyes shall see a quiet habitation." In crowded cities I often turn aside from the noisy thoroughfare, where some consecrated church stands open all the day and invites me to a moment of private prayer, like that of the publican in the Temple. I exclaim, "How awful is this place; none other than the gate of Heaven!" I see the altar where faithful priests "minister unto the Lord" as of old in Antioch,[1] and the sacred pale where the family of Christ kneel at the Holy Table to gather immortality[2] from the broken Bread and the chalice of the true Vine. There, too, is the "Volume of the Book" enthroned upon the lectern; the Everlasting Gospel borne, as on eagle's wings, to every kindred, and nation, and tongue; "whose leaves are for the healing of the nations."[3] And there, in "the seat of the elders," and everywhere, ready for the hands of worshippers, I see the Book of Common Prayer; that treasure of "gold, frankincense and myrrh," which we still open daily before the Lord, like the wise men who followed the Star of Bethlehem—those first fruits of the Gentiles who worshipped the Holy Child.

God send the day when in the unity of a restored Christendom, "one Lord, one Faith, one Baptism," we shall all be partakers of that "one Bread," and once more lift up our voices "with one accord," albeit with many tongues, in that incomparable language of the Creed: "I look for the Resurrection of the dead: and the Life of the world to come."

---

[1] Acts xiii. 1.   [2] St. John vi. 53–60.   [3] Rev. xxii. 2.

# THE REFORMATION PRAYER BOOKS.

# THE REFORMATION PRAYER BOOKS.

The line of thought which will guide me in discussing the subjects of precomposed prayers in general, and the Reformation Prayer Books in particular, is admirably laid down in the following words of the Acts of the holy Apostles; Acts ii. 42:

"And they continued stedfastly in the apostles' doctrine and fellowship, and in breaking of bread, and in prayers."

This description is given of the first believers by the Holy Ghost. This description supplies the criteria which accredit all believers, in every generation and in every age, who can justly lay claim to full communion with the company of the faithful, the Body of Christ, the One Holy Catholic and Apostolic Church.

The tests are few; only five in number.

*First.* Under *Apostolic* government.

*Second.* Holding "the faith once delivered unto the saints," without addition or depravation. The Apostles' *Doctrine.*

*Third.* In official association, in public

worship and spiritual life and conduct, with the Apostles or their representatives. *Apostolic Fellowship.*

*Fourth.* In scrupulous attendance upon, and reception of, the Blessed Eucharist as administered under the authority of the Apostles. *Apostolical Breaking of the Bread.*

*Fifth.* And in faithful participation in the public worship of the churches, as directed and guided by the forms prepared and enjoined by the Apostles. *Apostolic Prayers.*

These tests, or criteria, are very simple in character. The Apostolical ministry is an historical fact as fully and strongly confirmed by evidence as any fact in human experience. It involves, as embodying the gift of official spiritual life for all time to come, the principle of *succession;* since, so far as we know, all life in nature and in grace is continued in this way. The seed which we hold in our hand to-day is the product of last year's planting, and so we go back step by step, through seeds innumerable, to the gracious hand of the Great Parent of Life in the creation. You and I represent parents two in number, and they in turn each bring two into view,. and thus in succession we traverse the centuries until we come to those whom God made as the crowning act of creation.

The same principle perpetuates government of whatever kind, while it lasts, in the succession of its chief officer, holding and handing on the supreme office which embodies the gift of national life. This principle, so familiar—as meeting us everywhere in the field, in the home, and in the state—is appropriated by Almighty God in perpetuating His Church. The Apostles and their successors, immediately under Christ as their head, bring the gifts of *grace* to men, in an *official ministry*.

But as the treasure is so precious, as the gifts are of such transcendent importance, God guards their transmission with especial care. He overrules His Church to arrange that the parentage in the sacred ministry must be more than in natural descent. An earthly son counts *two* parents, a Bishop in the Church counts at least *three*. The security thus provided is complete. Humanly speaking, it is impossible that in such a succession there should be a failure.

The Apostolical government has been overthrown by Rome in an act of revolution. She put down and set aside the government of the Apostles as a *corporation*, and substituted the rule of one Apostle and his alleged successors, the Popes, as *a monarchy*.

The Apostolical government since the sixteenth century has been rejected by many who name the name of Christ, and they are living under systems of polity of their own invention. The *Apostles*, not one, but *all*, ruled the one Holy Catholic and Apostolic Church of Christ. The test is simple, and we challenge its application to ourselves.

We have brought this fundamental truth into view and emphasized it thus, because this test, "*the Apostles*"—the plural, *not one, nor none, but* ALL—this test gives validity and value to all the others: Doctrine, Fellowship, the Breaking of the Bread, and the Prayers. These are all the possession, so to speak, of the Apostles. We may read the passage quoted from Acts, to bring out its full meaning in this regard, as follows: "They continued stedfastly in (1) the Apostles' Doctrine, and (2) the Apostles' Fellowship, and (3) the Apostles' Breaking of the Bread, and (4) the Apostles' Prayers."

These features of the Gospel dispensation, the Kingdom of Christ—or, as we would say, of the Church—were all placed by the Divine Head under the government of the Apostles. And to qualify them to take the supervision and settle forever these necessary things, they were filled with the Holy Ghost, they were specially enlightened, strengthened and guarded, so that they could act, and teach, and formulate and establish what was necessary, without the possibility of mistake. They, the Apostles, were, for the purpose of prescribing the necessary things upon which the divine life of the Church depends for its continuance and perpetuation, *infallible.* The Holy Ghost made and kept them so. And in recognition of this fundamental truth, the appeal of the faithful, when they have felt themselves oppressed with tyranny or distressed by false teaching, has always been to the undivided and primitive Church—and ultimately to the Word of God, as interpreted by those in the first age who continued stedfastly in the Apostles' doctrine and fellowship, and in breaking of bread, and in prayers.

Committed then to the Apostles' jurisdiction by their Divine Master were doctrine, practice, sacraments and worship. And of these they took charge, and gave us in substance what we know as the Apostles' Creed; the communion of the faithful in religious life and association; the celebration of the Blessed Eucharist, and the Liturgy—which voices the celebration—and allied offices and prayers. These are their gifts under Christ to us; and the Holy Spirit puts upon these gifts His imprint, and stamps them as "Apostolical." Living men, from generation to generation and from age to age, hand those gifts on and down to us. They are an historical legacy—just as our life is a bequest from the past flowing down into us from our ancestors. These gifts are just as fresh and precious now as they were when the Apostles first conveyed them to men, even as our natural life now abiding in us is essentially what it was when it started on its career from Adam.

Our assigned duty is to discuss within certain limits of time, say between A.D. 1547 and 1662, the fortunes and vicissitudes of the *Apostolic Prayers* in our Anglican Communion.

My venerable predecessor in this course has told you the story of the Primitive Liturgies, flowing like the river of Paradise from *one* fountain in *fourfold* channels, and making glad the City of God.

It is my privilege to take up the narrative where he dropped the thread, and follow the fortunes of this divine gift, the Apostolic Prayers, through a period of little more than a century. The extremes of our survey are the accession of Edward VI., in 1547, and the first years of the reign of Charles II., in 1662.

The interval covers five complete reigns of kings and queens, the rebellion under Oliver Cromwell, and the beginning of a sixth reign, that of Charles II. The times were restless, unsettled, full of change. All things seemed like the troubled sea tossed to and fro. In Church and State, in manners and customs, at home and abroad, it was the same. The rejection of Papal domination in the reigns of Henry VIII. and Edward VI.; the return to it again in that of Mary; its rejection for a second time and finally when Elizabeth came to the throne in 1558; and then the repudiation of historic Christianity in the days of the Commonwealth —mark changes, not a few, in religion. In civil affairs, the transition from the absolute monarchy of Henry VIII. to constitutional liberty, secured by the Bill of Rights in 1688, was characterized by many and conflicting vicissitudes. The oppression of the Tudors was scarcely as intolerable as the selfish greed and cruelty of the factions who ruled the land under the boy King from 1547 to 1553; and the tyranny of the Stuarts was less odious than the canting hypocrisy of the Protector and his followers. Social and domestic life in these hundred years moved from old surroundings to new. The mediæval features which marked the home, the citizen, the soldier when the last Henry died, were all gone when the Savoy Conference gave us the last revision of the English Prayer Book in 1662.

In such an age of changes what are we to expect, or rather what are we to dread will take place in the Church of God? There are elements in her which must remain unaltered —if not, she ceases to exist. And we may well tremble for her safety, when we see the fabric of ecclesiastical government shaken to its foundations, and transitions rapid and startling from Roman to Reformed, and back again to Roman, and then reverting to Reformed once more to pass beyond the metes and bounds of Catholicity into individualism and negation—we may well tremble for the Church's safety, nay for her very existence, under such circumstances. She must preserve her polity, her faith, her loyal submission to authority, her sacraments and her prayers. Can she do this when such vicissitudes pass over the land? We answer she can, and she did; and the way in which this came about, guided by the protecting care of God, we proceed to show. On the preservation of the polity of the Church depended absolutely the preservation of all other necessary things, which are sheltered by that polity.

The English episcopate in the line of Canterbury knew no lapse during this unsettled period of transition and change. Cranmer succeeded Warham, and Pole, Cranmer, and

Parker, Pole; and then the succession follows without a break to our own Archbishop Benson of to-day. There was no interruption, and the Apostolic government continued through all the chances and changes of the eventful century and a quarter, during which the Prayer Book of our Mother Church was in the process of assuming its present form.

If the suggestion arises in your minds, that among the contingencies which might have occurred, was the adoption of extempore prayers, dismiss it at once and forever. Such a thing as extempore prayer in public worship is absolutely unknown to the historic Church of God. It is irreconcilable with the test of primitive discipleship, *"continuing stedfastly in the Apostles' prayers."* For it is not possible to continue in extempore prayer. The sound dies upon the ear, and the words are no more, except as a memory. And every repetition of extempore prayers on a fresh occasion of worship would only increase the difficulties, by confusing the impression with variations of the forms, and additions to the amount of matter.

The essential idea of *"extempore"* is, that it is fresh and new at the moment and springs spontaneously from the occasion. So that as time ran on, the Apostles' prayers—on the assumption that they were *extempore*—would accumulate and tax the memory of any one to recall them; and if he did, and continued stedfastly in them by using them, he would cease to follow the example of the Apostles, since he would reverse their practice, by reciting *precomposed* forms of prayer, while they poured forth their prayers without book or the aid of memory. It is impossible to continue stedfastly, we say, in extempore prayers. Prayers must be precomposed and be set down in some permanent form, for the use of those who are to *continue* in them.

And again, extempore prayer in public under the condition which our Lord prescribes—that "two or three" as a minimum *must agree* as touching what they ask—is absolutely excluded from the Church, unless the worshippers surrender themselves entirely into the hands of him who offers prayers. For, consider, in extempore prayer, if it be *really extempore*, the hearer cannot know what the speaker is about to say. Hence if he truly prays he must accept without reserve what is offered up to God by another, as his own. Prayer touches the deepest and most sacred things of our hearts; it covers the field of conscience, and gathers and presents to God the needs and cravings and fears of our moral and spiritual nature. How can we be sure that another and a stranger can know us as we know ourselves, and rightly represent us to the ear of God? We cannot, and hence we must listen and judge of what we hear, before we pray. But this is practically impossible. No two states of mind are more diverse than the critical and the devotional. In the former we are on the bench of the judge, we are weighing and considering, separating and deciding; in the latter we are on our knees as penitents and petitioners, the mind is in subjection to the spirit. As critics the mind rules; as devotees the spirit. We cannot, if we would, keep passing—as sentence after sentence falls upon our ears—from the critic's stool, if we approve, to our knees in devotion, and then in an instant back again as critics, to the seat of judgment. Such rapid and constant transitions from opposite poles of personal condition are impossible for any man. If it be urged in reply, "Oh! we know beforehand what our leader in devotion will offer in prayer;" then the answer is immediate—prayer in that case ceases to be extempore. And if we must have precomposed forms, the Apostles' prayers are better. The substance must be better, and the form as well. As to the substance, there is no need of change or variation except within very narrow limits; and these exigencies can easily be provided for, and are in all liturgies. The deep things of man's nature, the necessities of body and soul, are ever the same; they alter not from age to age. And hence the language of prayer is universal for all time and all men. God teaches us how to pray—directly in the Lord's Prayer, and indirectly in the primitive liturgies through the Apostles; and we shall do well if we continue stedfastly in their prayers. The form is better, since devotion has its technical language as well as science, and the original mould in which the form of prayer and praise is cast was prepared by the hand of God. Extempore prayer, therefore, in public, in the Church of Christ, is an incongruity so great, that it is not to be reckoned as a possibility that can happen, by those who remember what our Lord has said, and what His Apostles, as guided by the Blessed Spirit, have taught. The continuity of the Church, under the government of the Apostles and their successors in office, runs along the lines of faith, morals, sacraments and worship. The prayers form one of the strands which bind and hold the Church as one and identical from the day of Pentecost to the present hour, and everywhere throughout the world.

In the reign of Henry VIII. (1509-1547) when our survey begins, the English Church was still in her mediæval condition. In her ecclesiastical relations she was a national Church in association with other national churches of the West subject to the Patriarch of Rome.

Her insular position and distance from the centre of power had helped her sovereigns and people to assert and keep alive their independence to a degree that was elsewhere unknown, and prepared the way when occasion offered to lead them to break absolutely from the obedience of the Pope.

This occasion occurred when Henry was bent upon securing his divorce from his wife Katharine of Aragon. The Pope was personally ready to comply with Henry's wishes as to divorce, but he was coerced into refusal by Katharine's mighty nephew, the Emperor Charles V. of Germany. The English King, a thoroughly bad man, would not brook delay or endure contradiction; and so he led the estates of the realm to do what they were educated and ready to do—declare themselves as a national Church, free.

The pivot on which the English Reformation turned was the assertion of the principle of national independence in ecclesiastical jurisdiction and administration. The question proposed to the two Convocations of Canterbury and York—the legislative and governing body of the English Church—was this, "Hath the Bishop of Rome by divine right (jure divino) any more jurisdiction within this realm of England than any other foreign Bishop?" To this inquiry, after deliberation, the Convocations answered, with scarcely a dissenting voice, "No." The principle here asserted is universally true, and applies with equal force to every national Church, which either has been, or is, or may be subjected to the usurpation and tyranny of some exterior power. *This is the great principle of the English Reformation*, the principle which explains it and justifies it. It happened to be applied and successfully asserted in the reign of a selfish, sensual, bad King. His lust and brutality were the accident which prompted him, and spurred him on to suggest and sanction the measures which set his Kingdom ecclesiastically free from Rome. Without this liberation from the thraldom of the Pope, reformation in any true sense would have been impossible. Henry was the instrument in the hands of Divine Providence, to enable the English people, as a nation, to proclaim their autonomy in ecclesiastical affairs, and secure this independence by canonical enactment in Convocation, and legal statute in Parliament, with the consent of the Crown. The wrath of man was thus overruled to praise God.

The course of events in Henry's reign simply marks the process of legislation, which severed the connection, that was the growth of centuries, uniting England in a net-work of many strands with the See of Rome. Thus far, and thus far only, the Reformation advanced in the days of the eighth Henry. It was a *preparation* for reformation, rather than the Reformation itself. It was a clearing of the decks, and a cutting of the cables, which would enable the ship to be navigated and to sail away under the direction of her own lawful master and officers. This was done, and effectually done, prior to the accession of Edward VI., January 28th, 1547.

If we ask, what was the condition of the English Church when Henry breathed his last, we answer generally, it was mediæval still, save and excepting that it had renounced allegiance to the Pope. Its continuity with the past was unbroken. Cranmer had succeeded Warham as Archbishop of Canterbury, with the sanction of the Bishop of Rome; and under him the Church remained essentially the same in doctrine, fellowship, sacraments and prayers. No change was perceptible in service of worship; and the people gathered as they had been accustomed to do in their cathedrals, parish churches and chapels, to join in the same prayers and participate in the celebration of the same sacraments, as had been their habit since the Norman Conquest. The legislation of Henry VIII., as regards doctrine and public worship, had promised change, but effected little. Its course was marked by these enactments:

1. The Ten Articles touching religion, passed in the summer of 1536.
2. The Institution of a Christian Man, "the Bishops' Book," sent forth in 1537.
3. The Six Articles' law, enacted in 1539.
4. A Necessary Doctrine and Erudition for any Christian Man, known as "the King's Book," adopted in 1543.
5. The Litany in English, June 11, 1544.

These publications were attempts to popularize the teachings of the Church by exposition of some of her formularies, and to familiarize the people with certain portions of the service by translation. They varied in detail as to theological character, but not sufficiently to affect the truth of the general statement, that they were all thoroughly mediæval in their character. Their bearing upon the especial subject, which we have in hand, the history of the English Prayer Book, lies in this, that they rendered into English and explained the Lord's Prayer, the Ten Commandments and the Creeds, and other matters deemed necessary for a Christian man to know. They constituted a preparation, therefore, for the great achievement of the next reign, the compilation and setting forth by authority of the English Book of Common Prayer.

The essentials of public worship in our approach to God in prayer and praise in the Catholic Church, must continue always the same. The form may vary in language and arrangement; and indeed a moment's reflection will show that this must have been inevitable during a period of transition such as marked the settlement and formation of the nations of Europe in the greater part of the Middle Ages, say from A. D. 500 to A. D. 1300. For then nothing was fixed, nothing was settled. Language, customs, the surroundings and accidents of life at home and abroad were in a state of constant change. Hence the Church, as a matter almost of necessity, made use of the venerable language—which enshrined the literature of the Western world—in the public offices of religion.

The Churchman of the Middle Ages and of

Henry the Eighth's time, had no one book which would carry him through the entire services of the day, as is the case with us in our Book of Common Prayer. He must have, for example, his *Breviary* for daily offices; his *Missal* for the sacrament of the Altar; his *Manual* for the occasional offices which a priest could administer; his *Pontifical* for the services especially belonging to the office of a Bishop; and other books for minor offices, and the arrangements of the sacred seasons. He was, however, for the most part, at less disadvantage than we would at first suppose, when thus deprived of the constant aid of a guide in his devotions, since the scenic character of the services and the object lessons of the ritual kept him in close companionship with the holy rites of his religion.

The reign of Edward VI. (1547–1553) gives us, we may say, our present Book of Common Prayer—since the Book which we now use, just revised and enriched, is essentially the same Book which was set forth by authority in Edward's first act of uniformity, passed January 21, 1549. The successive revisions in England since that date have been *four* in number, those namely of 1552, in this same reign; of 1559, in the reign of Queen Elizabeth; of 1604, in the reign of James I.;

and the final revision at the Savoy Conference in 1662. This final revision emphatically brings into view, by its initial rubric, the ecclesiastical legislation of Edward VI., in 1548, as the guide in ritual for all time to come. The second year of that sovereign from January 28, 1548, to January 28, 1549, is selected as furnishing in rite and ceremony, in vestments and adornment, the example, which we must follow if we are obedient to authority in the celebration of public worship,

As preliminary to the setting forth of the Prayer Book in English, which was in course of preparation, "The Order of Communion" was authorized by royal proclamation, March 8, 1548, and continued in use until Whitsunday, 1549. In this Order the portions addressed to and for the use of the people were in their mother tongue, while the priest's part remained as before in Latin.

The first Prayer Book of Edward VI. was compiled and arranged and set forth by men, advanced in years in 1549, whose lives had been passed hitherto under the old regime, and who were imbued with the spirit of liturgical worship as they had known it from childhood. The Book was prepared for the use of a people, who had never known aught else than liturgic worship, and whose education and training had ever been in the use of the old service books. There go with this first Prayer Book of Edward VI., therefore, traditions and associations of the past which must be kept in view and taken into account in estimating its character. We must remember what the past had been as touching public worship, both on the part of those from whose hands we receive the precious gift, and of those for whose use it was primarily designed. This consideration—and it cannot be set aside —furnishes an interpretation to what else might be doubtful, and emphasizes with greater force what is clear, in its directions for practical use and its theological statements for instruction in doctrine.

The second Prayer Book of Edward VI., which was in use for only a few months (November 1, 1552, until the death of the young King, July 6, 1553), was due in its production to two facts, first the flight into England of numerous foreign refugees from Switzerland and Germany and the consequent strengthening of the extreme protestant or Zwinglian party; and secondly the deprivation and imprisonment of conservative Bishops and others, who would have opposed the radical spirit which was now in the ascendant.

Martin Bucer, Peter Martyr and others from the continent led the attack upon the first Prayer Book of Edward VI. The factions which ruled the land—the Somersets and the Northumberlands—cared for nothing save self-aggrandizement, and hence were ready to sanction anything which would subserve their personal ambition and their greed for wealth.

The chief grounds of assault against the Book were found in the Eucharistic Office, and the vestments. In the end the malcontents triumphed, and a second act of uniformity was passed in January, 1552, authorizing and enjoining a revised Book of Common Prayer; which was to come into use in the succeeding autumn, on the feast of All Saints. This Book records the low-water mark of the English Reformation; and hence, if we find, that with all its changes in the direction of Zurich and Geneva, it drops no essential principle of Catholicity, we may rest assured that the continuity of our Mother Church in the prayers as well as in the episcopal succession was never broken. This is the undoubted fact. First, the act of uniformity, which establishes the second Book, indorses the first in these words: "It is a very godly order, agreeable to the Word of God and the primitive Church, very comfortable to all good people desiring to live in Christian conversation and most profitable to the estate of this realm." Second, the many changes which appear in this Book in variation from its predecessor, are due to omission and transposition, rather than to substitution of new matter. There is, it is true, much in this Book, which a loyal Churchman laments, but there is nothing which need make him tremble for the preservation of the orthodoxy of our communion. It has been suggested, that Cranmer brought under the notice of the revisers the Mozarabic Missal, which is closely allied to the old Gallican use, and that thus the changes in the arrangement of the Communion Office, and of other parts of the new Book, can be explained. This is a reasonable conjecture, but whether true or not, the fact remains, that there is a likeness between our Prayer Book of to-day and the Gallican Liturgy.

The replacing an old Book with a new was not so rapid a process in those days (1552) as it is now, and as the feast of All Saints (November 1), 1552, was the date of the introduction of the second Book, and Edward VI. deceased on the 6th of July of the following year, there was scarcely opportunity for this revision to have reached the parish churches before the great change came when the Princess Mary became Queen, July 6, 1553.

The importance of the Book, however, lies not in the length of time it was in use, but in the fact, that it was chosen as the model after which the revision in the reign of Queen Elizabeth was made, in 1559; and in consequence it has influenced all subsequent revisions, and our own American Prayer Book.

The reign of Queen Mary (1553-1558) is a blank as regards our English Prayer Book, since she brought back the status of ecclesiastical affairs to what it was at the close of her father's (Henry VIII.) reign, 1547—save and excepting the rehabilitation of the monasteries, which Henry had dissolved, and the restoration to their owners of the Church lands, which her father and half-brother had forcibly alienated. But Mary's reign chronicles one fact which must be noted, namely, that the Church's continuity was not broken—although she brought England back to its mediæval position of submission to the Pope. The Roman authorities waited until Archbishop Cranmer was executed, before Cardinal Pole was placed in the See of Canterbury. There was no break—the Pope, even after all that had occurred, recognized Cranmer's position; and Pole succeeded when his predecessor was dead, and not till then. The Church, in her flow of life, had passed thus far without interruption, from the episcopate of Archbishop

Warham to that of Pole. The conflict had been, and was, between the old and new service books in use in the land. There were as yet not two rival Churches in England. There were two schools in the one national Church; and now for five years the cause of the old triumphed over the new. The submission to Rome was an accident, deplorable of course, but still an accident which did not destroy the Church's life. She lived on and carried the nation with her as one communion until the twelfth year of Queen Elizabeth, when Rome by formal act withdrew her subjects from the Church's altars and set up rival and schismatic altars of her own. Then, in 1571, the English people became divided; and formal schism from the Church of England for the first time appeared when the Pope excommunicated the Queen, released her subjects from their allegiance, and commanded those who were willing to obey to forsake their Mother Church—which alone held canonical jurisdiction in the land—and submit to his usurped authority. While Henry, and Edward, and Mary reigned, there was but one Church in England. Nor were there two until Elizabeth had been upon the throne for twelve years, and then the sin of schism was begun by Rome, and has been continued by her ever since. Meanwhile Cardinal Pole had died, within a day of Queen Mary, in 1558, and Archbishop Parker had succeeded, and all the functions of ecclesiastical life had passed without interruption to him, to be transmitted by him to others until, we trust, the end of time.

With Queen Elizabeth (1558–1603), came the final triumph of the new service books over the old. Her act of uniformity carrying with it her Prayer Book, was passed in 1559. The second Book of Edward VI. was chosen as the basis of revision. This pacified the extreme Protestants, while the changes in the direction of primitive and Catholic use reconciled the conservatives—and the third English Prayer Book was established by law, June 24, 1559.

The changes were few but important. The Ornaments Rubric brought the Church back in externals to the second year (1548) of Edward VI. The combination of the words of administration of the Holy Communion employed in the two Books of Edward, and the omission of the Black Rubric upon kneeling at reception, asserted doctrinal truth which had been obscured in the Book of 1552. This Book, with very slight changes which were made at the Hampton Court Conference and enjoined by James First's act of uniformity in 1604, remained in use for nearly one hundred years, until the reign of Charles II. in 1662—with the exception, of course, of the period of the Protectorate of Cromwell, when all liturgical services were banished from the land.

The settlement under Queen Elizabeth establishes and fixes the uninterrupted continuity of the English Church, from the remotest antiquity to that date, upon a basis of historic evidence which cannot be shaken. This continuity in office, in doctrine, in prayers, is the first and great principle of the English Reformation. A national Church the English Church had ever been. Magna Charta in its first article proclaimed her *free*, and she had not been backward in making good this proclamation of her freedom, in her relations with the Patriarch of Rome. She had acknowledged him as the *administrative* head of Christendom, but beyond that point she would not go; and when his demands exceeded what was reasonable and just she successfully resisted them. At length, as we have seen, the occasion was supplied on the part of Henry VIII. to sever absolutely her connection with Rome, and the three estates of the realm—Parliament, Convocation and the Crown—concurred in the action, and the English Church was free. The temporary return to submission to papal authority under Queen Mary (1553-1558) did not in the least compromise the national character and constitution of our Mother Church of England. Indeed, up to the Vatican Council of 1870, the national autonomy of the Churches owning obedience to the Roman Patriarchate was never in essence lost. The Gallican liberties, for example, were not a myth, but a reality, even within the century now closing; and the Uniat Churches on the eastern borders of Europe illustrate the truth of this statement.

The English Church reformed herself from within, on constitutional and canonical lines. Archbishop Parker was as truly the successor of Augustine as were Pole, Cranmer and Warham. And under him, as representing Apostolical polity, were sheltered and sanctioned doctrines, morals, sacraments and prayers.

The Apostolical succession, so scrupulously guarded and preserved through the reigns of Henry, Edward, Mary and Elizabeth, furnishes an irrefutable answer to the charge of *schism;* and the retention of the three creeds and the explicit endorsement and recognition of the four ecumenical councils constitute a sufficient reply to the allegation of *heresy*.

Our fortunes are bound up with those of our Mother Church; and hence we may look back with satisfaction to her foundations exposed to view through discussion and contention for full thirty years (1529–1559) in the heart of the sixteenth century. Polity, doctrine, sacraments and prayers survive the violent convulsions and vicissitudes of these stormy days; and the continuous flow of the Church's life, in her fourfold channels, is never interrupted or dried up, but runs right on and down to more peaceful years when dangers are past. And now it comes to us, with its treasures of priceless worth for time and for eternity.

The last revision of the English Prayer Book occurred in 1662, on the accession of Charles II. at the Restoration. The basis of revision was, of course, Elizabeth's Prayer Book of 1559. This was strengthened, in the direction of the explicit assertion of positive truth. The Bishops and theologians of 1662 had learned wisdom from their ancestors of 1552, and from the terrible experience of the last eleven years under the Commonwealth; and they naturally turned away, with stern resolve, from Geneva, and faced Catholic antiquity. For example—to be specific in a few instances. In the title to the Absolution, and in other places where the priestly office is necessary for the valid performance of rite or act, the word "Minister" is replaced by the word "Priest." In the Communion Office the first oblation of the bread and wine was enjoined; the rubrics relating to the manual acts in the consecration of the

Blessed Eucharist were inserted; and the rubrics which direct the Priest how he shall consecrate more bread and wine, and how he shall reverently care for what remains of the consecrated elements, were added. And the Ornaments Rubric, which was borrowed from Elizabeth's act of uniformity, and which stands as the general law governing the externals of the Church of England in her fabrics and clergy, was amended to make it more clear and explicit, and was retained in its place at the beginning of the Book. It reads as follows: "And here is to be noted that such ornaments of the Church and of the Ministers thereof at all times of their ministrations shall be retained and be in use as were in this Church of England by the authority of Parliament in the second year" [January 28, 1548—January 28, 1549] "of the reign of King Edward the Sixth." These illustrations will serve to show the spirit of the teaching embodied in the present Prayer Book of our Mother Church of England.

The revision of 1662 may be justly called the *last*, because no changes of any moment have been made since by the orders-in-council; which have necessarily been issued, on the accession of successive sovereigns—and by the Amendment to the Act of Uniformity passed in the reign of Queen Victoria. The Church of 1662, therefore, has been from that date and is to-day the *ecclesia docens* of England. When we took our departure as an independent daughter Church, we brought our Mother's Prayer Book with us, and used it, as far as local circumstances would allow, as our own. This fact we explicitly declare in the Preface of our Prayer Book, since we affirm in unmistakable language as follows : "This Church is far from intending to depart from the Church of England in any essential point of doctrine, discipline or worship, or further than local circumstances require."

Our Prayer Book, therefore, is a blessed memorial of the past, replete with interest which centres in, and gathers around, no other book save the Bible. Indeed, the Prayer Book gives expression to the Bible. It is the Bible's voice ; it is the Bible in action. The Prayer Book, in the use of the congregation, makes the Word of God vocal in supplication and praise. The Prayer Book, in the hands of the Priest and people, is the instrument for the celebration of sacraments and holy rites, the performance of acts which the Bible enjoins as of perpetual obligation. The heart of the Prayer Book is the Communion Office, because in the celebration of that holy sacrament we "do show forth the

Lord's death till He come;" and this exhibition of Calvary carries us back to the sacrifice of Abel, and forward to the vision of "the Lamb slain from the foundation of the world," the Lamb in the midst of the throne. This service is the centre around which all else is grouped. The other services lead up to it, and are related to it, in the ideal of the Christian life. Baptism, Catechism, Confirmation, are steps to the Lord's Table. The daily offices are a lesser communion, and Holy Matrimony and the Visitation of the Sick and the Burial of the Dead, lack something if the Blessed Eucharist does not crown them with its benediction.

The sacrifices of the law—the burnt offering, the peace offering and the sin offering—looked forward to the one "full, perfect, and sufficient sacrifice, oblation, and satisfaction, for the sins of the whole world," which was offered upon the cross. "The Apostles' prayers" enshrined the service which commemorated the sacrifice of Calvary, and applied, by the power of the Holy Ghost, the benefits of the Atonement to the worthy recipient. The Law passed into the Gospel, in the Breaking of the Bread and in the prayers of the Apostles; and these we have in our Office for the administration of the Holy Communion. This is the heart, therefore, of our Book of Common Prayer, as it has ever been in essence the heart of all worship. Here we have, beyond all doubt, the echo of the voices of those who had heard our Lord say, "Take, eat; this is My Body. Drink ye all of it; for this is My Blood." And in succession ever since, without intermission, at stated intervals living men, authorized to act and speak in the Lord's name, have continued to break the Bread and to pray, down to our own time and to us. What a wonderful book our Common Prayer Book is! It lies upon our tables or is held in our hands like any other book; but, unlike any other book, it springs into life and has voice and action when God's people pray to Him and praise Him, and when priest and congregation join in the celebration of sacraments and sacred functions. What a wonderful book our Common Prayer Book is! It connects us by hand joined to hand of living men who have used the essentials of its offices, to the birth day of the Church of Christ, when the Apostles began, with the first believers, to celebrate the holy mysteries in the breaking of the Bread, and to offer the prayers. What a wonderful book our Common Prayer Book is! It brings the future into view, in some details, even to the end of time. Changes many and great may take place, and almost all things may wear a different aspect, but here in our Book of Common Prayer we have fixed realities, we have things which will not, which cannot change. We have Baptism, and Confirmation, and the Holy Communion. We may look forward into the dim and distant future, and though we may be certain of very little on other lines of prophecy and promise, yet along those which our authorized spiritual guide-book lays down, we are sure of what will come to pass. Our children are within view, and their children may appear before our eyes close in death; but in imagination we may go on picturing to ourselves unborn generations, filling with life the centuries yet to be, and among them and for them, our posterity however remote, will abide the blessings treasured up in our Book of Common Prayer. Let us then be loyal to its teaching, and faithful in its use. Let us not compromise the priceless truth, which it puts in our possession as a sacred trust, for our own instruction and a legacy for our children. Let us remember, that those who form the front rank of believers in Christ, and on whom the light of the Blessed Spirit shines in the Word of God, revealing them to us as examples, are described as continuing "*stedfastly* in the Apostles' doctrine and fellowship, and in the breaking of bread, and in prayers."

This word *stedfastly* belongs to those Pentecostal believers. Let us strive to make it ours as well. Let us hold our Prayer Books firmly in our hands. Let us refuse to listen to voices which would fain persuade us to play fast and loose with truth, to evade it, and explain it away. Let us ever bear in mind that our Book of Common Prayer is a *positive* Book. It affirms truth in the spirit of love clearly and explicitly. It teaches us to say "I believe, I believe." All around us the air is full of evasions, interpretations, negations: all around us men are saying "I don't know," "I doubt," "I don't believe," "I can't accept this." Alas, stedfastness was never born of doubt, evasion, negation; it is made of sterner stuff; it is the essence of true manhood; it must rest on solid foundations—and these foundations our Prayer Book places beneath our feet in the creeds and sacraments and means of grace. Our foundation is Christ, and He is the subject of our Book of Common Prayer. Let us then be stedfast, like the first believers, and uphold the teaching and practice enjoined by our Prayer Book, by leading lives answerable to our profession. You have yet to read and learn how our American Prayer Book was revised a century ago, and how in the present year it comes to us once more revised, and enriched, and completed, and, so to speak, sealed for use without further change we trust for a very long time to come. As you read the chapters which succeed, the conviction will deepen within you, I am sure, that as a Church we have hitherto continued stedfastly in the Apostles' prayers.

# EARLY AMERICAN PRAYER BOOKS.

# EARLY AMERICAN PRAYER BOOKS.

It is most fitting that, in connection with the consideration of the Standard Prayer Book of 1892, we should consider the liturgical work our fathers did, and the guiding principles which gave us the Prayer Book of our first hundred years of life and growth. Within the walls of Christ Church, Philadelphia, there gathered, day after day, the Churchmen of 1785 and 1789, debating, first, the changes rendered necessary to make the services "conformable to the principles of the American Revolution and the Constitutions of the several States"; and, secondly, the further alterations in the Book of Common Prayer which took shape in the "Proposed Book;" and then, in 1789, the practical return to the English Prayer Book as a model and guide in forming our present book. We may well and wisely review the work thus done. At our entrance upon a second century of autonomous existence; at the period in our history when the labours of a decade and more of years of liturgical study and legislation have resulted in the adoption of a new Standard; we may profitably recall the story of the earlier revisions, and review in the light of a century's experience the measures and men of 1785 and 1789.

A score or more of foolscap sheets, soiled and stained with age, largely in the handwriting of William White, and displaying the cramped, abbreviated style of writing he so uniformly employed, record the "Acts of the Convention of 1785." Of these, "The Alterations agreed upon and confirmed in Convention for rendering the Liturgy conformable to the Principles of the American Revolution and the Constitutions of the Several States," afford us the results of the first attempt of our fathers at a revision of the Book of Common Prayer. It is certainly characteristic of the patriotic White, as well as thoroughly consonant with the environment of the revisers of 1785, that this first American liturgical document should begin with words such as these:

"That in the Suffrages, after the Creed, instead of *O Lord, save the King* be said, *O Lord, bless and preserve these United States.*"

The Churchmen of 1785 were patriots; and the shaping of our services as we have them in the Book of Common Prayer we have used for a hundred years, was done by the very men who, in the halls of Congress or on the field of battle, won for us our independence. It was the first expression of the autonomy of the American Church—this breathing to the God, who had given us our nationality, of the Church's prayer for the benediction and preservation of the United States!

Following this patriotic aspiration were directions for the omission of the prayers for the reigning family of Great Britain, in the morning and evening services; the omission of the suffrages of the Litany for the king and royal family; and the substitution, in place of the suffrages on behalf of parliament, of the petition, "That it may please Thee to endue the Congress of these United States, and all others in authority, legislative, executive, and judicial, with grace, wisdom, and understanding, to execute justice and to maintain truth." For the Prayer for the High Court of Parliament prescribed in the English Office when the Litany was not read, a Prayer for Congress was set forth. The Collect for the King's Majesty was changed so as to comprehend "all in authority, legislative, executive, and judicial, in these United States." The Collects for the king in the Communion Office were omitted, or similarly changed. In the answer in the Catechism to the question "What is thy duty towards thy neighbour?" the words, "To honour and obey the king," were changed so as to read: "To honour and obey my civil rulers." In place of the observance of November 5th, January 30th, May 29th, and October 25th, a Service was appointed to "be used on the 4th of July, being the anniversary of Independence." In the Forms of Prayer to be used at Sea, the "United States of America" took the place of the reference to "our most gracious Sovereign Lord King George and his kingdom," and the word "island" gave place to "country." The words, "O Almighty God, the Sovereign Commander," were omitted, and "the honour of our country" was substituted for "the honour of our sovereign."

These changes were a necessity. At the breaking out of the war, the clergy who continued to use the state prayers in the service were subjected to interruption and insult, and often to personal peril. As the wish for independence took shape in the minds of the people, the clergy were forced to face the problem of ceasing their public ministrations, or of omitting these obnoxious prayers. In Christ Church, Philadelphia, the first formal and authoritative change in the services took place, ere had ceased the echoes of its chimes, ringing in—responsive to the pealing of the State

House bell—the proclamation of liberty to the world. On the 4th of July, 1776, the vestry of this church, from among whose worshippers and pew-holders fully half a dozen of the "signers" were furnished, met, and ordered the omission of the prayers for the king and royal family.[1] The Virginia legislature, by formal vote, took the same step the following day. The vestry of Trinity Church, Boston, on

---

[1] The action of this Vestry, taken at a meeting held at the house of the Rector, the Rev. Jacob Duché, D.D., on the night of the fourth of July, 1776, was the first official recognition, given by any public body, to the nationality of the United States. It may be truthfully said, that the American Church was thus foremost in recognizing the American State. The original record of this event, in the minutes of the Vestry, is carefully preserved in the archives of Christ Church. The resolution adopted reads as follows : "Whereas, the honorable Continental Congress have resolved to declare the American colonies to be free and independent States, in consequence of which it will be proper to omit those petitions in the Liturgy, wherein the King of Great Britain is prayed for, as inconsistent with the said declaration, Therefore, resolved that it appears to this Vestry to be necessary, for the peace and well being of the Churches, to omit the said petitions ; and the rector and assistant ministers of the united Churches are requested in the name of the Vestry and their constituents, to omit such petitions as are above mentioned."—ED.

the receipt of the news of the Declaration of Independence, requested their rector—the excellent Parker, afterward the second Bishop of Massachusetts—to omit the same prayers. Elsewhere this course was followed, either by vestry-vote or in glad recognition of the fact so often asserted by our fathers, and expressed in their own language in the preface to our Book of Common Prayer, that, "When, in the course of Divine Providence, these American States became independent with respect to civil government, their ecclesiastical independence was necessarily included." We may then, in this connection, seek to emphasize the historic statement, that in Christ Church, Philadelphia, and by the formal act of its constituted authorities, the Prayer Book of our fathers was first adapted to the change in the civil relations of the people, and the freedom of the American Church from the duty of recognizing an alien ruler and a foreign domination first fully asserted to the world. Honour, then, is rightly due to the vestry and people of the united congregations of Christ Church and St. Peter's, who were thus the pioneers in the work of American liturgical revision.

Bishop White tells us that at the assembling of the Convention of 1785 in Christ Church,

Philadelphia, few if any of the delegates contemplated other or further changes in the Prayer Book than were necessary to make its language conform to the altered condition of civil affairs. The fundamental principles first formulated in White's own statesman-like essay on *The Case of the Episcopal Churches Considered*, and clearly enunciated at the preliminary Convention of 1784—held in New York, and more generally attended than the meetings prior to the second Convention of 1789—expressly limited the alterations of the liturgy to those rendered necessary by the civil independence already secured. In Connecticut and throughout New England, and, in fact, to a large extent in New York and New Jersey, the clergy and laity deemed themselves incompetent to undertake the revision of the liturgy while destitute of the episcopal order. So widely did this principle obtain that the Assembly of Virginia restrained the clergy by specific enactment from consenting directly or indirectly " to any alterations in the order, government, doctrine, or worship of the Church." It was but natural then, that the earliest representative gathering of American Churchmen from the various States laid down as a principle of the Church's organization, that it "shall maintain the doctrines of the Gospel as now held by the Church of England, and shall adhere to the liturgy of the said Church, as far as shall be consistent with the American Revolution and the Constitutions of the respective States."

Even as late as May, 1785, the Convention of Virginia, untrammelled by the "fundamental principles" of the meeting in New York in 1784, gave an unwilling sanction to a review of the Prayer Book, accompanying its assent with the requirement of the use of the English book "with such alterations as the American Revolution has rendered necessary."

In the interval between the preliminary meeting of 1784, in New York, and the gathering in Christ Church, Philadelphia, of the Convention of 1785, Seabury had been consecrated by the Scottish Bishops for Connecticut, and had been enthusiastically welcomed to his see by the representative Churchmen of New England and New York. At his first Convocation, held a few weeks before the meeting in Philadelphia, in the autumn of 1785, the Bishop of Connecticut, with the Rev. Samuel Parker, of Trinity Church, Boston, afterward Bishop of Massachusetts; the Rev. Benjamin Moore, afterward Bishop of New York, and the Rev. Abraham Jarvis, Seabury's successor in the see of Connecticut, gave careful consideration to the matter of Prayer-Book alterations; but their action was confined to the changes deemed necessary to accommodate the Prayer-Book services to the civil constitution. "Should more be done," writes Seabury to White, in giving an account of the Middletown Convocation, "it must be a work of time and great deliberation." A Convention of the churches of Massachusetts, New Hampshire, and Rhode Island, held in September, 1785, ratified the omissions and alterations agreed upon at Middletown, and postponed action on other proposed changes till after the Convocation appointed to meet at New Haven, and the Convention about to convene in Philadelphia.

Few more notable gatherings than that assembled in Christ Church, Philadelphia, in September, 1785, are recorded in our ecclesiastical annals. Sixteen clergymen and twenty-one laymen, of whom five clergymen and thirteen laymen were from Pennsylvania, and one clergyman and six laymen from Delaware, formed this body, which organized under the presidency of William White, with the Rev. David Griffith, of Virginia—Washington's friend and rector—as Secretary. It is safe to assert that whatever may have been the results of this meeting, the rector and representatives of Christ Church, Philadelphia, certainly shaped its measures and largely influenced its decisions. Within these very walls, consecrated to Church and country—where, a year before, the first ecclesiastical convention or council composed of laymen as well as clergymen known in ecclesiastical history had convened, it was fitting that the organization of the Church at large should be attempted. In this venerable church, after deliberations and discussions occupying the careful thought and the earnest prayer of some of the foremost men of the time in Church and State, the foundations of the autonomous American Church were laid broad and deep. On these foundations was wisely, firmly, prayerfully, built the City of our God. Of these shapely stones was erected the fair structure, compactly fashioned, of the American Church. Within Christ Church walls, and under the overarching roof of this sacred fane, the corner-stone of our ecclesiastical system was laid.

The Convention of 1785 ratified and adopted the alterations of which we have already spoken, as required by the changed conditions of civil affairs. But while this was the limit of its liturgical revision, so far as any formal or authoritative legislation was concerned, the Convention at the very outset assigned to the committee appointed to report the alterations contemplated by the fourth fundamental principle, adopted by the New York meeting in 1874, the consideration of "such further alterations in the liturgy as may be advisable for this Convention to recommend to the consideration of the Church here represented." The names of this committee are those of the leading churchmen of the time. The clergymen were Provoost, of New York, afterward bishop; Abraham Beach, of New Jersey, one of the earliest to move in the matter of the organization of the American Church; White, of Pennsylvania, whose duties as president of the Convention practically prevented his service on the committee; Wharton, of Delaware, the first convert of the American Church from the Roman obedience; William Smith, removed from the charge of the College and Academy of Philadelphia, and now President of Washington College, Chestertown, Md., and Bishop-elect of the Church in that State; Griffith, afterward Bishop-elect of Virginia; and Purcell, a brilliant but erratic clergyman of South Carolina. Of the laity there were the Hon. James Duane, of New York, a patriot and statesman; Patrick Dennis, of New Jersey, a man of character and note; Richard Peters, of Pennsylvania, a scholar, a jurist, and a vestryman of Christ Church; James Sykes, of Delaware, who had won distinction in the war; Dr. Thomas Craddock, of Maryland, a man of high character and wide influence; John Page, one of Virginia's most noted sons; and the Hon. Jacob Read, of South Carolina, a leading patriot and publicist of his native State.

The pages of the Journal contain little information as to the debates in committee or in Convention attending the preparation of what is known in liturgical history as the "Proposed Book." Bishop White, in his *Memoirs of the Church*, adds but brief details to the scanty information which may be gathered incidentally from the manuscript memoranda and the unpublished or printed correspondence of the time. The changes finally agreed upon, comprising a thorough review of the Liturgy and Articles of Religion, were "proposed and recommended" for adoption at a subsequent Convention. The alterations were reported to the committee we have named by a sub-committee, of which the Rev. Dr. William Smith was the leading spirit. We have the testimony of Bishop White that they were not reconsidered in the committee to which they were reported, and that even on their presentation in Convention "there were but few points canvassed with any material difference of opinion." They were chiefly the work of the Rev. Dr. William Smith, whose preëminent part in this task of revision received the grateful acknowledgments of the Convention. To him, in connection with the Rev. Drs. White and Wharton, the publication of the Proposed Book was assigned. A wide liberty in the matter of further emendations or corrections was entrusted to, or certainly exercised by, the committee, and the published correspondence of its members—carefully preserved by Smith and issued within the last few years by authority of the General Convention—is the chief source of our knowledge of the principles guiding the proposed revision, and the changes adopted as the volume passed through the press.

With only marginal notes of the omissions and additions which had been approved; correcting in manuscript the English books already in use, and with the manuscript schedule of changes suggested and proposed—a document still extant, and in its cramped chirography, with all its interlineations, corrections, erasures, fac-similed as one of our earliest liturgical authorities—the Convention, as a body, concluded its work of revision. There was no time or opportunity during the progress of the work of revision by the Convention, for putting these changes authoritatively in print. Still, the Daily Morning Service, as proposed by the committee, was used on the closing day of the Convention. The Journal records, under date of Friday, October 7, 1785, as follows:

"The Convention met, according to adjournment, and attended Divine Service in Christ Church; when the Liturgy, as altered, was read by the Rev. Dr. White, and a suitable sermon was preached by the Rev. Dr. Smith, after which the Convention adjourned, etc." For this sermon Dr. Smith received the thanks of the Convention. In referring to the work of revision, he alludes in his discourse to the work of the Convention as that "of taking up our Liturgy or Public Service where our former venerable Reformers had been obliged to leave it; and of *proposing* to the Church at large such further alterations and improvements as the length of time, the progress in manners and civilization, the increase and diffusion of charity and toleration among all Christian denominations, and other circumstances (some of them peculiar to our situation among the highways and hedges of this new world) seem to have rendered absolutely necessary."

In this hasty revision, as adopted in Convention or published to the world by the

Committee, additional sentences were prefixed to the Order for Morning and Evening Prayer; the word "Absolution" was omitted from the rubrics in the Daily Office; grammatical changes were made in the Lord's Prayer; the use of the *Gloria Patri* was limited to its recital at the end of the "Reading Psalms;" in the *Te Deum* in place of "honourable" was substituted "adorable, true, and only Son," and for the phrase "didst not abhor the Virgin's womb" was inserted "didst humble Thyself to be born of a pure Virgin;" the choice of Psalms and Lessons was left at the discretion of the minister; in the Apostles' Creed the article "He descended into hell" was omitted; the Nicene and Athanasian Creeds were omitted; the suffrages after the bidding to prayer were abbreviated; the lesser Litany was shortened; for archaic words modern equivalents were substituted; verbal changes were made in the various Offices; parents were allowed to be sponsors; the omission of the sign of the cross in baptisms, when particularly desired, was authorized; the phrases "I plight thee my troth," and "With my body I thee worship," and "pledged their troth either to other" in the Marriage Service were omitted; in the Burial Office the restriction as to the use of the service in the case of those unbaptized was removed; the form of absolution in the Visitation Office was omitted and the "declaration" in the Daily Offices substituted in its place; a form of prayer, etc., for prisoners, agreed upon by the Irish archbishops, bishops, and clergy in 1711, was adopted with modifications, such as the substitution of the "declaration" for the absolution, and the omission of the short collect, "O Saviour of the world," etc.; in the Catechism the reply to the question, "When did you receive this name?" was changed as follows: "I received it in baptism, whereby I became a member of the Christian Church;" instead of the words "verily, and indeed taken" in the explanation of the sacraments, was substituted the phrase "spiritually taken;" the number of the sacraments was expressly limited to "two, Baptism and the Lord's Supper;" a special prayer was substituted to be used after the General Thanksgiving instead of the Service for the Churching of Women; the Commination Office was omitted, the three collects being placed among the occasional prayers; twenty only of the XXXIX. Articles were retained, and these were pruned and modified in their language; for the Psalter there were inserted selections arranged for the morning and evening services for thirty days; some of the Psalms were wholly omitted and others considerably abbreviated, the design being to obviate the necessity of reading in public the "imprecatory" passages; a service was prepared for the Fourth of July; eighty-four selections of Psalms in metre were added, and fifty-one hymns; four leaves of tunes, with the notes engraved, were added at the close of the work. The title of this rare volume, of which four thousand copies were issued, but of which only a few still exist, is as follows:

"The BOOK of COMMON PRAYER, And Administration of the SACRAMENTS, And other RITES and CEREMONIES, As revised and proposed to the Use of the Protestant Episcopal CHURCH, At a Convention of the said CHURCH in the States of New-York, New-Jersey, Pennsylvania, Delaware, Maryland, Virginia, And South-Carolina, Held in Philadelphia, from September 27th to October 7th, 1785. PHILADELPHIA: Printed by HALL and SELLERS: MDCCLXXXVI."

This work was reprinted in London in 1789, and was highly praised in a critical notice in the *Monthly Review* (vol. 80, p. 337). It was reprinted in the Rev. Peter Hall's *Reliquiæ Liturgicæ*, and within the last few years again and again as one of the documents of the "Reformed Episcopal Church." The original is one of the costliest as well as rarest of the ecclesiastical "Americana" of the period.

The Proposed Book, after many and vexatious delays, at length appeared in print. Its reception, complete and in binding, is recorded by Dr. Smith in a letter addressed to Dr. White under date of April 29, 1786. Its publication awakened no enthusiasm, and it was soon evident, to quote the testimony of Bishop White, "that, in regard to the Liturgy, the labors of the Convention had not reached their object." Even the committee entrusted with the preparation of the volume for the press felt and confessed the imperfection of their work. "We can only, in the different States," writes Dr. William Smith to the Rev. Dr. Parker, of Massachusetts, under date of April 17, 1786, "receive the book for temporary use till our churches are organized and the book comes again under review of Conventions having their bishops, etc., as the primitive rules of episcopacy require." South Carolina, Virginia, Maryland, and Pennsylvania proposed amendments to the committee's work. No Convention met in Delaware, and consequently no action respecting the book was taken. New Jersey formally rejected the proposed revision, and memorialized the General Convention of 1786 with respect to "the unseasonableness and irregularity" of the alterations made by the committee of publication without the "revision and express approbation of the Convention itself."

The Convention of New York postponed the question of the ratification of the Proposed Book, " out of respect to the English bishops, and because the minds of the people are not yet sufficiently informed." The prospect of the success of the efforts of the Convention of 1785, for securing the episcopate in the English line of succession, served materially to hinder the ratification and general use of the Proposed Book. The objections urged by Bishop Seabury and the New England Churchmen to its adoption seemed cogent and convincing when echoed by the English archbishops and bishops. Some of the most glaring defects in this hasty and ill-considered revision were obviated by the action of the Wilmington Convention of 1786. The mutilation of the Apostles' Creed, and the rejection of the Nicene Symbol were now no longer insisted upon. The omitted clause, " He descended into hell," was restored to the Apostles' Creed, and the Nicene Creed was replaced in the Daily Offices. The temper of the times was becoming conservative. Catholic truth, as held by Seabury and the Churchmen at the North, was no longer decried. The crudity and incompleteness of the proposed revision was confessed by all. It practically died in the effort that gave it birth.

The action of the Wilmington Convention in removing the objections of the English archbishops and bishops to imparting the succession to the American Church, sealed the fate of the Proposed Book. Its use had never been general, and in all but a few churches it was now forever laid aside. In New England, its adoption by Trinity Church, Boston, was only temporary. At Trinity, Newport, R. I., the attempt to introduce it, we are told by Bishop Seabury, was productive of consequences threatening the very life of the parish. Connecticut never admitted its use in any of its churches, and in New York the influence of Provoost was insufficient to secure its general introduction. It was used for a time in Christ Church, Philadelphia, as in numerous churches in the Middle and Southern States, but its omissions and alterations were generally distasteful, and it was, in all cases, after a brief time laid aside. The clergy returned to the use of their old office books, the changes being noted in manuscript, as in the case of the Christ Church Prayer Books of the day, still religiously preserved, and showing the alterations made to render the service conformable to our civil independence and the constitutions of the independent States.

On the eve of the Convention of 1789, under date of June 20 of that year, Bishop Seabury gave fully and without reserve his criticisms on the Proposed Book to his episcopal brother of Pennsylvania:

> Was it not that it would run this letter to an unreasonable length, I would take the liberty to mention at large the objections here made to the Prayer Book published at Philadelphia. I will confine myself to a few, and even these I would not mention but from a hope they will be obviated by your Convention. The mutilating the Psalms is supposed to be an unwarrantable liberty, and such as was never before taken with Holy Scriptures by any Church. It destroys that beautiful chain of prophecy that runs through them, and turns their application from Messiah and the Church to the temporal state and concerns of individuals. By discarding the word Absolution, and making no mention of Regeneration in Baptism, you appear to give up those points, and to open the door to error and delusion. The excluding of the Nicene and Athanasian Creeds has alarmed the steady friends of our Church, lest the doctrine of Christ's Divinity should go out with them. If the doctrine of those Creeds be offensive, we are sorry for it, and shall hold ourselves so much the more bound to retain them. If what are called the damnatory clauses in the latter be the objection, cannot these clauses be supported by Scripture? Whether they can or cannot, why not discard these clauses, and retain the doctrinal part of the Creed? The leaving

out *the descent into Hell* from the Apostles' Creed seems to be of dangerous consequence. Have we a right to alter the analogy of faith handed down to us by the Holy Catholic Church? And if we do alter it, how will it appear that we are the same Church which subsisted in primitive times? The article of the *descent*, I suppose, was put into the Creed to ascertain Christ's perfect humanity, that he has a human soul, in opposition to those heretics who denied it and affirmed that this body was actuated by the divinity. For if when he died, and his body was laid in the grave, his soul went to the place of departed spirits, then he had a human soul as well as a body, and was very and perfect man. The Apostles' Creed seems to have been the Creed of the Western Church; the Nicene of the Eastern, and the Athanasian to be designed to ascertain the Catholic doctrine of the Trinity, against all opposers. And it always appeared to me, that the design of the Church of England, in retaining the three Creeds, was to show that she did retain the analogy of the Catholic faith, in common with the Eastern and Western Church, and in opposition to those who denied the Trinity of Persons in the Unity of the Divine Essence. Why any departure should be made from the good and pious example I am yet to seek.

There seems in your book a dissonance between the offices of Baptism and Confirmation. In the latter there is a renewal of a vow, which in the former does not appear to have been explicitly made. Something of the same discordance appears in the Catechism.

Our regard for primitive practice makes us exceedingly grieved that you have not absolutely retained the sign of the Cross in Baptism. When I consider the practice of the ancient Church, before Popery had a being, I cannot think the Church of England justifiable in giving up the sign of the Cross, where it was retained by the first Prayer Book of Edward the VI. Her motive may have been good; but good motives will not justify wrong actions. The concessions she has made in giving up several primitive, and I suppose, apostolical usages, to gratify the humours of fault-finding men, shows the inefficacy of such conduct. She has learned wisdom from her experiences. Why should not we also take a lesson in her school? If the humour be pursued of giving up points on every demand, in fifty years we shall scarce have the name of Christianity left. For God's sake, my dear sir, let us remember that it is the particular business of the Bishops of Christ's Church to preserve it pure and undefiled, in faith and practice, according to the model left by apostolic practice. And may God give you grace and courage to act accordingly!

In your Burial Office, the hope of a future resurrection to eternal life is too faintly expressed, and the acknowledgment of an intermediate state, between death and the resurrection, seems to be entirely thrown out; though, that this was a Catholic, primitive and apostolical doctrine, will be denied by none who attend to this point.

The Articles seem to be altered to little purpose. The doctrines are neither more clearly expressed nor better guarded; nor are the objections to the old Articles obviated. And, indeed, this seems to have been the case with several other alterations: they appear to have been made for alteration's sake, and at least have not mended the matter they aimed at.

That the most exceptionable part of the English book

is the Communion Office may be proved by a number of very respectable names among her clergy. The grand fault in that Office is the deficiency of a more formal Oblation of the Elements, and of the Invocation of the Holy Ghost to sanctify and bless them. The Consecration is made to consist merely in the Priest's laying his hands on the elements and pronouncing, *"This is my Body,"* etc., which words are not consecration at all, nor were they addressed by Christ to the Father, but were declarative to the Apostles. This is so exactly symbolizing with the Church of Rome in an error;—an error, too, on which the absurdity of Transubstantiation is built,—that nothing but having fallen into the same error, themselves, could have prevented the enemies of the Church from casting it in her teeth. The efficacy of Baptism, of Confirmation, of Orders, is ascribed to the Holy Ghost, and his energy is implored for that purpose; and why he should not be involved in the consecration of the Eucharist, especially as all the old Liturgies are full to the point, I cannot conceive. It is much easier to account for the alterations of the first Liturgy of Edward the VI., than to justify them; and as I have been told there is a vote on the minutes of your Convention, *anno* 1786, I believe, for the revision of this matter, I hope it will be taken up, and that God will raise up some able and worthy advocate for this primitive practice, and make you and the Convention the instruments of restoring it to His Church in America. It would do you more honour in the world and contribute more to the union of the Churches than any other alterations you can make, and would restore the Holy Eucharist to its ancient dignity and efficacy. . . .

Hoping that all obstructions may be removed by your

EARLY AMERICAN PRAYER BOOKS. 101

Convention, and beseeching Almighty God to direct us in this great work of establishing and building up the Church in peace and unity, truth and charity, and purity, I remain with great regard and esteem,
Your affectionate Brother and very humble Servant,
SAMUEL Bp. Connect.[1]

No more able or convincing arguments could have been prepared. The words of Seabury in this *critique* are worthy of the closest reading, the most careful consideration. They give us in calm and temperate language the plea of the New England churches, and their spiritual head, for the primitive faith and order, and the Catholic use.

In 1789 the General Convention of the churches in the Middle and Southern States again convened in Christ Church, Philadelphia, but the desire for unity dominated in every mind the wish for liturgical changes or omissions. To the episcopate of Seabury, secured in 1784 from the Catholic remainder of the Church in Scotland, had been added the English succession conferred on White and Provoost at Lambeth, in 1787. The churches of the New England States recognized Seabury as their head. The churches of the Middle States

---

[1] First printed in Perry's *Hist. Notes and Documents*, pp. 386–388, forming Vol. III. of *The Reprint of the Early Journals*, 1785–1835.

and those at the southward were united in their acceptance of the episcopate as received from the Mother Church of England. To bring together the long-parted and oft-times contending Churchmen of the North and South was the desire of well-nigh every heart. Through the mediatorial offices of Parker, of Massachusetts—seconding and furthering measures recommended and approved, if not first suggested, by William White—this blessed union and comprehension were happily effected. The steps taken at the first Convention of 1789, held, as so many of our noteworthy ecclesiastical assemblages have been from the first, in Christ Church, Philadelphia, resulted, on the occasion of the second gathering of the Church in Convention in the same place and the same year, in the welcoming of Seabury and the New England deputies to what was now in its fullest, truest sense a *General* Convention of the Church in the United States. In the State House, in the apartments of the General Assembly of the Commonwealth of Pennsylvania, to which the General Convention had adjourned the day before, on Friday, October 2, 1789, by the signing of the amended Constitution, changed with this end in view, by Seabury and the New England deputies, the American Church was at length at unity in herself.

The revision of the Liturgy was now a primary duty. The Proposed Book does not appear as a factor in the revision of 1789, which gave us the Prayer Book we now, after a century's use, lay aside for the Standard of 1892. Bishop White had also written to Seabury under date of May 21, 1787, that "if it should be thought advisable by y$^e$ general body of our Church to adhere to y$^e$ English Book of Common Prayer (y$^e$ political parts excepted), I shall be one of y$^e$ first after y$^e$ appearance of such a disposition, to comply with it most punctually.

"Further than this, if it should seem y$^e$ more probable way of maintaining an agreement among ourselves, I shall use my best endeavours to effect it. At y$^e$ same time, I must candidly express my opinion, that y$^e$ review of y$^e$ Liturgy would tend very much to y$^e$ satisfaction of most of y$^e$ members of our communion, and to its future success and prosperity. The worst evil which I apprehend from a refusal to review is this, that it will give a great advantage to those who wish to carry y$^e$ alterations into essential points of doctrine. Reviewed it will unquestionably be in some places, and y$^e$ only way to prevent its being done by men of y$^e$ above description, is y$^e$ taking it up as a general business."

Seabury had written to Parker, of Boston, under date of February 13, 1788: "I never thought there was any heterodoxy in the Southern Prayer Book, but I do think the true doctrine is left too unguarded, and that the offices are—some of them—lowered to such a degree that they will, in a great measure, lose their influence."

It was, therefore, with the full approval of the men who certainly occupied representative positions in the churches both of the Northern, the Middle, and the Southern States, that the "Proposed Book" was laid upon the shelf at the meeting in 1789. The New England deputies, under the lead of Dr. Parker, of Massachusetts, who voiced the views and wishes of Seabury, "proposed that the English book should be the ground of the proceedings held, without any reference to that set out and proposed in 1785." Others contended that a liturgy should be framed *de novo*, "without any reference to any existing book, although with liberty to take from any, whatever the Convention should think fit." The result of this discussion, so far as the House of Deputies was concerned, is seen in "the wording of the resolves as they stand in the Journal, in which the different committees are appointed, to prepare a Morning and Evening Prayer, to prepare a Litany, to prepare a Communion Service," and the same in regard to the other offices of the Prayer Book. The phraseology employed in 1785 was to *alter* the services respectively. The latitude of change this action of the House of Deputies seemed to justify, was essentially modified by the general disposition of the Convention to vary the new book as little as possible from the English model, and the further circumstance that the House of Bishops "adopted a contrary course."

To this House of Bishops, meeting in the Committee Room of the House of Assembly, and later, when "the public service" required the use of this apartment, in the Apparatus Room of the College of Philadelphia, after divine service each day in Christ Church or at the College Chapel, and consisting only of Seabury as Presiding Bishop, and William White—Provoost being absent—is due much of the conservatism and Catholicity of the revision of 1789 as contrasted with the abortive attempt of 1785. The alterations, other than those of a political nature which had been earlier agreed upon, were mainly verbal, with the omission of repetitions. Additions were made to the Occasional Prayers; Selections of Psalms were inserted ; and the Office for the Visitation of Prisoners, from the Irish Prayer Book, was retained. A Form of

Prayer and Thanksgiving for the Fruits of the Earth was adopted—thus, first of all Christian bodies in this land, nationalizing the Thanksgiving observance. Forms of Prayer for Family Use, condensed from those of Bishop Gibson, were inserted. Besides these changes, Bishop Seabury obtained the restoration to the Prayer of Consecration in the Holy Communion Office, of the Oblation and Invocation found in King Edward VI.'s first Prayer Book and retained in the Scotch Office.

In this notable improvement of the Liturgy, Seabury secured for the American revision of 1789 a closer conformity in the Eucharistic Office to primitive models, and fully met the requirement of the *Concordat* he had signed with the Scottish bishops on his elevation to the episcopate.

It is thus that there has come down to us from the primitive days, the prayers of the saints, in the form and manner we have used them in our public devotions for a hundred years. Ours is the heritage of prayer coming from the historic past, and the very history of revisions and changes has an interest and value all will confess. "The prayers of my mother the Church," cried the dying George Herbert—"there are no prayers like hers." And we, conscious of what was secured to us by the men and measures of 1789, may thank God for the gift to us of that incomparable book of devotion which, with the slight changes and enrichments of our own revision, will, as we fondly believe, be to us in the years to come what our fathers' book of 1789 has been to us for the first century of our independent life. For the revision of 1789—both for what it was and for what it superseded—we may ever thank our own and our fathers' God.

# THE PRAYER BOOK ENRICHED.

# THE PRAYER BOOK ENRICHED.

THE subject which is assigned to me is in a way the easiest, and in a way the most difficult, of the four subjects. It is the easiest, because it deals with questions so recent and so fresh in all our minds as to require only the recall of things with which we are virtually familiar. It is the most difficult, because it lacks the charm of antiquarian research, and has to do rather with surface matters than with questions that lie in the deeper waters of history and doctrine.

It will be remembered, that in the Convention of 1880 a resolution was introduced into the House of Deputies in the following language: *"Resolved,* That a joint committee, to consist of seven bishops, seven presbyters, and seven laymen, be appointed to consider, and to report to the next General Convention, whether, in view of the fact that this Church is soon to enter upon the second century of its organized existence in this country, the changed conditions of the national life do not demand certain alterations in the Book of

Common Prayer in the direction of liturgical enrichment and increased flexibility of use."

It is a very striking fact, that the Convention of 1889—at which a considerable number of changes were finally adopted, and at which all changes that have now been made were acted on for the first time—synchronized entirely with the beginning of the second century of the organized existence of the Church in this country. For it was on October 2d, 1889, the actual centennial anniversary of the day when the three bishops met first in Christ Church, Philadelphia, and organized the Upper House of the General Convention, that the opening service of the late General Convention was held in St. George's Church, New York, and the two houses met for organization.

And it is a coincidence not to be omitted from our thoughts, that the completed Prayer Book is established in what is called the "Columbian" year : so that it becomes us, I think, to bear in mind that a service in the English tongue, after the manner of the English Church, was the first that consecrated to God the soil of this North American continent. In the name of his sovereign, Henry VII., Sebastian Cabot took possession of the new-found land, which he called Prima Vista—the first seen—and held a religious service there, and sailed from that northern point perhaps as far as Florida,-the Prima-Vera lands of constant Spring. So that neither to Roman nor to Spanish influence in speech or faith, but to the religion and the language of the Anglo-Saxon people, are due the opening of the new world in which we live, and the bringing of that new land into subjection to Christ our Lord.

It is inevitably suggested by the language of the resolution, that we appointed the joint committee to trace out the course of action along the three lines : the changed conditions of the national life, liturgical enrichment, and increased flexibility of use.

The changed conditions of our national life would make sufficient theme in themselves. In this Columbian year, when we are observing that which approaches most nearly to antiquity in this new world, the hundred years of ecclesiastical existence seem comparatively short. And yet not only has the national life grown from the sparse rootings of the great Puritan settlement in New England, and the small and scattered seed of Church of England people and Roman Catholics in Maryland and Virginia, into our great and seething mass of only partially assimilated nationalities; but the Church herself has grown from a *very* "little one," struggling with every possible hindrance and antagonism, into a position where, not perhaps in numbers, but certainly in influence ecclesiastical and religious, and in power of both intellect and wealth, it is almost the dominant religious feature in our national life. And this Church stands to-day, I believe, before a vista of increasing influence, which adds intense solemnity to every action that is proposed in regard to her formularies of order and worship. It seems to me, that the changed conditions of our national life, so far as they affected the action of the committee on the revision of the Book of Common Prayer, ran in two directions. In the first place, the time had come when certain timidities that marred the action of the Convention which set forth the first book, had grown into the courage of taking what was good which had been left out then, and restoring it to its rightful place. Perhaps the most marked illustration of this was in the honesty which withdrew all right to omit from the old Creed the article, "He descended into hell"; and the reconsideration of the curious and unreasoned fear which had omitted from Evensong the hymn *Magnificat*, lest, somehow or other, it should seem to imply a worship of the Blessed Virgin Mary.

These two great gains in truth and worship mark progress in our national and ecclesiastical life. Other than this, I do not think we have accomplished all that we might have done. I think there should have been a service appointed for the Fourth of July, the keeping of which ought certainly to be observed more generally than it is, with more religious recognition of the great Christian duty of patriotism; and in some better way than by the imitation and importation of the barbarous noises of a barbarous nation. We have gained a special service for the "Harvest Home"; I wish we might have had some prayer for the country as well. But I am glad that in the Evensong, in the prayer for those in authority, we have got back the statement which impresses upon rulers "Whose authority they bear," and upon the ruled, the recognition that is due to the powers which "are ordained of God." The careful provisions for dividing and shortening the services, are no unimportant concession, beside, to the changed conditions of our modern life.

It has been my privilege to be associated with the work of the committee on the revision of the Book of Common Prayer during the twelve years of its existence, serving first under the always inimitable chairmanship of our Presiding Bishop, and afterwards as chairman of the committee since 1886. And I desire to bear witness to the fact, that the members of the Commission have approached their work with the fullest sense of its difficulty and delicacy; with the deepest possible reverence for the marvellous compilation they were called to revise; and with an earnest purpose not to mingle any common clay with its pure gold, or to weave any threads of coarse and common stuff into the exquisite embroidery of Holy Scripture, and of words that have been, not only selected by trained liturgical scholars, but also hallowed by the reverent use of so many centuries. We felt what Stedman has so strongly said, that the ritual of our Episcopal Prayer Book is "the most wonderful symphonic idealization of human faith,—certainly the most inclusive, blending in harmonic succession all the cries and longings and laudations of the universal human heart invoking a paternal Creator. . . . Upon its mystic tide of human hope, imagination, prayer, sorrows, and passionate expression it bears the worshipper along, and has sustained men's souls with conceptions of Deity and immortality throughout hundreds, yes, thousands, of undoubting years. . . . In various and constructive beauty as a work of poetic art it is unparalleled . . .

as a piece of inclusive literature it has no counterpart, and can have no successor."

The very first thought that occupied the minds of the Commission was to restore lost treasures, because there could be no such liturgical enrichment as that which would reset old jewels in the crown. And while the last Commission has not felt itself bound to follow out the resolution adopted at the very first meeting of the original Commission, to touch nothing that could seem to affect doctrine, it must be plain to anybody who studies the result as it is now finally presented, that neither in the way of diminution nor addition have any doctrinal changes been introduced.

The first proposition in 1880, as I remember, struck almost everybody with a sense of suspicion and alarm. There are great numbers of people in this world to whom any large and strong proposition of this sort suggests at first sight one or the other of two things. And it has been rather curious to notice how this suspicion and alarm have lingered on for twelve years in minds of very different constitution, and for reasons very widely apart; have hindered and hampered more or less the progress of the work, by a combination of entirely opposite opinions against certain phases of it; and have succeeded, not in preventing the general purpose, but in seriously marring its perfectness.

*The suspicion* which haunted the minds of many men, certainly until the first report of the committee was made, was that some secret gall of vagueness and vapidity was concealed under the language of the resolution. And in spite of all the evidence of results, in spite of an acknowledgment all round that the work has been done in no narrow and partisan interest, a certain number of individuals in the Church held aloof for a long while from, what I believe that now even *they* acknowledge in the main to have been, a sound progress in the direction of liturgical improvement. The alarm which filled the minds (not unnaturally) of the most respectable and venerable body of men, to whom the mere fact of long attachment and association had so endeared the precise shape of the American Book of Common Prayer, that they could not brook the thought of the dotting of an undotted *i*, or the crossing of an uncrossed *t*, was that they feared the change would make unfamiliar the beloved features of what had come to be linked in with all the holiest memories of their lives.

We had to contend at first, also, with a third element—smaller, but not *therefore* less loud in its utterances—of people who desired larger and more sweeping changes, and opposed the more moderate proposals of the various committees, in the hope that this movement being made a failure, room would be made for them, by and by, to carry out their views. In spite of all this, and more and more as the work went on, agreement with wonderful unanimity has been reached in regard to the most important changes which the committee proposed.

We owe, I think, to a combination of feelings of this sort, the loss of certain things which, if they could have been secured, would have made the book more perfect than it is. I speak of them first, because, if this is to be historic record, I should be glad to have it known, that not only the Commission but the House of Bishops are on record in favor of the introduction of the English Versicles after the Lord's Prayer at Matins *and* Evensong; of the change of the expression in the Prayer for All Conditions of Men, to read, "the good estate of the Catholic Church"; of the permission to use the Ninety-fifth Psalm as an alternative form for our present *Venite ;* of the right to use the thanksgiving, "Thanks be to Thee, O Christ," after the Gospel. More serious, even, I think, than these, was the failure to adopt the authorized Collect, Epistle, and Gospel for use when the Holy Communion is celebrated at the time of a burial. And it is greatly to be regretted, it seems to me; because in the growing use of the Holy Communion in connection with burials, which will not and cannot be arrested by this negative action of the House of Deputies, we have failed to seize the opportunity of giving ecclesiastical authority and suggestion for the kind of service that is to be used. I think it matter of very serious loss, that the Prayer of Humble Access was not transferred to its much more natural position, which it holds in the Scottish Communion Office, namely, immediately before the act of administration of the consecrated Elements, instead of immediately before the act of Consecration.

There is no need, of course, to argue these things now; because the wise conclusion has been reached to make no further change, but to take the book as it is now and leave it, as I think it will be left, for many a year. But both as matter of history, and for the credit of the Commission that had the work in charge, it seems to me just and right to make the simple statement of these facts; and I think it ought to go on record also, that both in the Conventions of 1886 and 1889, whatever was adopted in the House of Bishops was adopted with practical unanimity, and in the House of Deputies with only a very small minority opposed; that out of thirty-three resolutions proposed by the Commission in 1883, only nine were lost entirely; that of the one hundred and forty-eight separate propositions which they contained, one hundred and nine were either finally adopted in 1886 or approved. And I go back with infinite thankfulness to the closing scenes of the Convention of 1883, when, in the crowded church, and with the largest representation of dioceses continued to the end that I have ever seen, the vote on the adoption of the committee's amended report was made most emphatic in its practical unanimity, as diocese after diocese was called, and answered aye.

Of the fifty-two resolutions approved in 1889, only seven were not adopted in 1892; and two of these losses are real gains, because one of them secures the use of the great Messianic Sixty-ninth Psalm on Good Friday; and the other removes even the appearance of approving the thought of evening ordinations and celebrations of the Holy Communion. And it is to be added, here, that the spirit of this last Convention in dealing with the final adoption of the Standard Book of Common Prayer has been more admirable than ever before, the concurrent action of the two houses more uniform, the majority of votes approaching more nearly to unanimity. And the book itself, with the accessories of printing so perfectly done as to make even the outward appearance worthy of its invaluable contents, will stand as a monument of that sort of reverence to the worship of our Blessed Lord which hesitates not to break the "alabaster box" of precious ointment, "very costly," so that its richest and its best may be offered as a token of adoring love.

For the first time in the history of the American Church the Standard Book is really a *book,* and not an *edition;* and the shrine is not unworthy of the jewel which it contains.

It would be very easy to make a sort of catalogue *résumé* of the results of the revision of the Book of Common Prayer. I am disposed rather to go on the principle of selection and classification.

Clear out above other gains, to me, stands the reparation we have made, in completing the list of the festivals of our dear Lord, by making full provision of services for the keeping of the great Feast of the Transfiguration—marred not a little, and diminished somewhat in its value, by the unreasoning and unfortunate position it is made to occupy in the Christian year; because it surely ought to have come somewhere in Epiphany time, and surely ought not to have come at a time of the year, when so many of our congregations are scattered to the four quarters of the world. Nevertheless it is true, that it has been vouchsafed to us in the American Church, to dignify this marvellous manifestation of our dear Lord's deity, into its due position of ritual observance in the Christian year. It completes the round of the marked events in the Master's life. It brings into prominence all the blessed lessons connected with it; the complete unveiling of the Divinity shining through the flesh in which our King was pleased to tabernacle while He was here on earth; the splendid intimation of the character of the Lord's risen body to-day, into whose glory the bodies of our humiliation are one day to be changed; the witness of the Law and the Prophets to Christ; the communion in the future world among the living and the dead, and between both quick and dead with Him; the seal set upon the power of the habit of real fasting and true prayer, to transfigure the coarseness and commonness of our natures here, and to bring us into closer communion with the dear Lord. All these are truths of infinite value and consolation, which on this feast, as its constant keeping among us will more and more go on, are emphasized and enforced in ways that cannot but be helpful to a fuller and more perfect acceptance of the faith.

Next to this, it seems to me, has been the great gain of the restoration of the three evangelical canticles to our Matins and Evensong. The mutilated *Benedictus* no longer jars upon our reverent sense of the completeness of inspired words; and the *Magnificat* and *Nunc Dimittis* have come back to their time-honored place in the evening worship of the Church of God. I am bound to say, too, in this same connection, that I think a great step forward has been taken in teaching people the rightful reverence that is due to Holy Scripture, in the complete wiping away from our liturgical use, of those curious mosaics of Psalms which were singularly unauthorized, unmusical, and unedifying; and in substituting, for the ten Selections—in which equal liberty was taken to mutilate the Psalms as they stand in Holy Scripture—a fuller set of Selections, in which the Psalms are all complete, except in the single instance of the old Compline Psalm. I believe, too, that the very admirable selection of Proper Psalms, for other days than the six for which they were appointed before, is a step in the direction of opening up to people—what often has seemed hidden—the Christian application of the Psalter, and the power of its adaptation to meet, not only the various incidents in the story of the Christian year, but also the varying demands and necessities of our individual lives.

In dealing with the Creeds, the Church has planted herself upon strong and unmistakable ground. In the first place she has put back into the Apostles' Creed the word "again," which is not only the true translation of the Latin word, but is the emphasis of the reality and identity of the resurrection body; and, in the next place, she has removed all accusation—which lay, not altogether unjustly, against her once—of tampering with an article of the Catholic faith, by removing the permission, which had been guardedly given, to omit from the Creed the article of the descent into hell. Not less clear and not less Catholic is the new rubric, which requires that the Creed commonly called the Nicene, shall be used after the Gospel on the five great feasts of Christmas, Easter, Ascension, Whitsunday, and Trinity Sunday; carrying with it the implication, correct in ritual and growing in use, that the Nicene Creed should be reserved for the Communion Office, and that the Apostles' Creed is the baptismal symbol and the right form to be used in Morning and Evening Prayer.

The removal of the *Gloria in Excelsis* from Morning Prayer, is a case of conformity to what I think has become the habit of our congregations. Its retention in the Evening Office, is in the line with certain Oriental uses of considerable antiquity and authority; but the true meaning of it is, I think, that the great hymn is relegated to find its most rightful and correct use in the Office of the Holy Communion. The same rule, I trust, will grow more and more into observance as applied to the shorter—which is, of course, the stronger—absolution; that it should be reserved for the faithful in the course of their preparation for the reception of the Blessed Eucharist. It is a most curious instance of mistaken choice, that because the Declaration of Absolution contains the positive statement of the power and commandment given to the priest to forgive the sins of the penitent—which some people do not like to believe or to say—therefore that which is a mere statement has more doctrinal significance and more actual power than the shorter form, which is the direct conveyance of the gift.

One must recognize, too, in the revised Prayer Book, distinct and definite gains in the restoration of the old idea of the vigil of certain Holy Days, by the authorized use of the Collect on the eve of the feast; in the provision of alternate Collects for the two great Feasts of Christmas and Easter; in the permission to omit the Decalogue at either of two celebrations; in the new Offertory Sentences, which seem so beautiful, that one only wonders that they have not been used before; in the *Kyrie* after the Summary of the Law; and in the change of the Prayer of Consecration, which makes a good grammatical sentence out of what certainly could not have been considered such before.

The story of the new rubric is one that is rather long to tell. The original proposition, forbidding any celebration without the presence of communicants, which was adopted by the House of Bishops, was not concurred in by the House of Deputies. I do not think that any particular theological opinion is to be argued from this want of concurrent action, because there was immediate and almost unanimous action in the House of Deputies, upon the rubric which the Bishops sent down—"And sufficient opportunity shall be given to those present to communicate." The single desire, so far as I know, either of the committee or of the bishops, was to prevent the separation of two things, which, by the very revealed description of the Blessed Sacrament, are two sides of the one great truth ; namely, that it is something to be *eaten* as well as *offered;* and that the Sacrifice must be partaken of, if those *by* whom it is, and *for* whom it is offered, are to derive the benefits for which the Holy Communion was instituted by our Lord.

To have secured the relegation of the preface in the Confirmation Office to its original and proper position of a rubric, by making its reading permissive and not obligatory; and to have thrown into the Office the Scriptural authority for Laying on of Hands, in the reading of the appointed Lesson, are two points of gain in the right direction ; not all, perhaps, that could have been desired ; but tending certainly to impress upon people the truth, that the confirming of vows is only the preliminary, human, and conditional part of the being confirmed by the Holy Ghost.

Nor do I feel that I ought to stop here, in the catalogue of enrichments, without noting that we have gained some opening Sentences with reference to the seasons of the Christian year ; an Offertory anthem at the presentation of the alms and oblations ; the Versicles—adapted somewhat—from the English Book in the Order for Daily Evening Prayer; the Collect for the Unity of God's People; Collects for

Rogation Sunday, the Rogation Days and for Missions; the Thanksgiving for a Child's Recovery from Sickness; and the penitential office for Ash Wednesday, giving the Fifty-first Psalm its proper place, as the great penitential psalm; and adding the beautiful Collect from the English Book, asking the pitifulness of the great mercy of God to loose those who are tied and bound with the chain of their sins.

We have made gains, too, in the addition of prayers which may be used in the Burial Office; one of which ties a new knot between our Prayer Book and the first book of Edward VI., and between the American Church and the dear old Mother Church of Scotland, to whom we owe not the episcopate only, but the primitive and un-Roman fullness of the Consecration Prayer in the Communion Office.

To me, the insertion in the Marriage Office of the words from the English book is not only a great enrichment, but a most valuable emphasis and endorsement of what seems, at any rate, to be an almost forgotten fact, namely, that in both the Jewish and the Christian dispensations, Almighty God has set His seal upon the honorableness and indissolubleness of the estate of marriage.

In these days, when marriage is degraded to

an unsanctified and unbinding civil arrangement, every public statement that asserts its Divine and primitive origin, and keeps about it all its sacred sanctions, is worth preserving. As we have had it hitherto, it might seem to be an Apostolic institution, originating with St. Paul, or with the author of the Epistle to the Hebrews; whereas it has its three great seals from the Father, the Word, and the Holy Ghost; from God, and Christ, and the Church—in the primeval Paradise, in our Lord's human ministry, and in the Apostolic days. And when men have learned that it is not only honorable but a "mystery"—which is the Greek word for a sacrament—in which the oneness of the flesh of the twain is involved, and which sets forth the organic and mystical union of Christ and His Church, there will be found some holy ground to stand on, against the theory of a mere civil contract in marriage, and against the degrading and disgraceful frequency and facility of divorce.

The question of increased flexibility of use, which was the other matter referred to the Commission, has been dealt with in various ways. We have in many instances only made lawful that which had become habitual, although with no other law than that of frequent use and of unwillingness on the part of the ecclesiastical authority to interfere with such use.

The absolute separation into three distinct parts, of the Morning Prayer, the Litany, and the Holy Communion; the authority to use the Litany in the evening; and the freedom given to the minister, subject to the direction of the Ordinary, to compile, out of the Book of Common Prayer, special offices on any day when Morning and Evening Prayer shall have been said, are the first instances of making flexible that which has been rigid, without opening the way to the license of mere parochial or individual selection. In the same direction, the permission to shorten Evensong by the omission of the Exhortation, and of all the prayers after the Collect for Grace; and while retaining the essential features of our Morning Prayer, to use only a sentence and the Lord's Prayer before the *Venite*, ending the Office with the Prayer for the President; these, with the authority at either celebration of the Holy Communion, when there are two celebrations, to omit the recitation of the Ten Commandments—always providing that the Summary of the Law be read when the Commandments are not—are steps in the direction of a flexible use which will not lead to the disuse of the Prayer Book.

In connection with this shortened Order for Morning Prayer when it immediately precedes the celebration of the Holy Communion, attention ought to be called to what Bishop Sparrow defined as the "rationale" of the Prayer Book. It involves, it seems to me, the teaching that the especial features of Morning Prayer are observed when the Lord's Prayer, the Invitatory Psalm, the Psalter for the day, the two Lessons, the *Te Deum* and *Benedictus*, the Creed and the three Collects have been used. And, next, it involves the principle that the rest of the service may safely be omitted, *because* the Office for the Holy Communion contains its own Confession and Absolution, its own highest act of thanksgiving, and, in the Prayer for Christ's Church Militant, the supplication for rulers and for "all conditions of men."

I am by no means clear that the time is not coming, when this Church will find itself wise in rising to the necessities of its great national possibility, to deal a little more freely even than we have with our Offices of Morning and Evening Prayer. If the question arises, as it seems likely to almost at any time, how we can meet the desire of the great Protestant bodies about us for some communion with us in the matter of worship; if, for instance, the day should come when we shall not only receive, as we are receiving, ministers trained in the various denominations into the Ministry of this Church, but when their congregations shall follow and come with them, it will get to be a serious question, whether we ought not to allow for such as these—and if for these, of course for those among us who may desire it— some larger liberty in the matter of the Offices which do not directly affect the sacramental doctrine and the sacramental grace.

It does not seem to me that it would be any breach, or would involve the risk of any breach, of our maintenance of the faith, in the only way in which it can be maintained, by the constant and quickening breath of definite liturgical worship, if we left ourselves somehow free, only to insist upon such Offices or parts of Offices as contain the essential sacramental elements of service. If we anchored ourselves firmly to the Offices for Holy Baptism and the Holy Communion and for Confirmation, the Ordinal, and the Marriage Service—so far as it asserts the Christian doctrine on the subject —I cannot but think, that, to those who are not trained to the majestic dignity of our Daily Order of Matins and Evensong there might be relaxation as to their use. I should greatly hope that such a course might tend to impress upon those to whom the Church's system ought to be more of a reality than it is, that we, who have by birthright the inheritance of this great system of prayer and praise, should practise it far more thoroughly than it is practised now.

And I cannot but believe that the time is coming, when even more than we have done now—in the printing of the Book of the Articles with its separate heading—may be done, to show that the XXXIX Articles, valuable as many of them are, are not intended even for our own lay people; much less for those who, from other religious bodies, are looking toward some recognized relation to us.

So far as this chapter is meant to be, and had to be, a somewhat dry historical *résumé* of results, I might well stop here; but there are two points which it seems to me need urging. In the first place, however one may have been at times distressed by the momentary differences or by outbreaks and evidences of warm opposition, I do not think any one of us can fail to thank God infinitely, not merely for the results, but, in the main, for the spirit and the manner in which these results have been attained. It seemed at first sight to many people dangerous to the last degree, to trust such a body as our General Convention has grown to be, with the delicate and difficult duty of altering the Book of Common Prayer. But the outcome has proved that those fears were groundless. The amount of time and thought and intense sense of responsibility; the intelligent interest, not more of the clergy than of the laity; the process of education in Liturgics; the unusual unanimity with which the main results have been secured; the great patience of the Church at large during the transition period, which has been prolonged beyond the first intention; and the emergence from the difficult and anxious questions which were connected with such a movement, with no effect produced but increased unity, intensified love and reverence for our precious heritage; the absence of any marring of its beauty, and the restoration of much treasure that had been temporarily laid aside: all these, certainly should make us feel most deeply that the time had come when the movement was not only needed, but when the work could be done. And while I think it is true, that what is commonly called the *jus liturgicum* does rest with the bishops; so that if any work of this kind is to be undertaken again it would be wise to provide by canon for what has been the fact by courtesy—namely, that the finished scheme should be prepared by the Bishops and then presented to the House of

Deputies—it has been very plain that, dealing under the solemn sanctions of the only authority under which we could act, and under the solemn surroundings of the marked presence of God, all has been overruled to His greater glory and His highest service.

And the second thing that needs, it seems to me, to be said, is that there ought to be more thoroughness and more faithfulness in the use of this book about which we talk so much, but which, it seems to me, too little forms and fashions either the teaching of the clergy or the religious character of our lives. There can be no question but that St. Paul meant to teach us a wholesome and important lesson when he said, not that the form of sound words was delivered to us, but that we were delivered into a form of sound words; that the object, that is to say, of Creeds and liturgies is to mould the devotional and doctrinal, and, consequently, the religious character of us all.

The Book of Common Prayer is, in itself, a system not only of worship but of training. It sets us poles apart from all modern theories about the education of a Christian child. Beginning with the implanted life of regeneration, the child is held steadily and step by step, along the plainly marked way of teaching and of worship, by which its whole life shall be moulded. It is never left in any doubt as to the certainty of its sonship of God. It is never left to any uncertainty as to its training for the kingdom of Heaven. And it is never without the constant reminder that, whether birth and inheritance ever are to meet, depends entirely upon the character, which we form by the grace of that birth, and which only can fit us for the enjoyment of that inheritance. The taught Catechism, the habit of prayer and church-going, the early Confirmation, and, consequently, the early coming to the Holy Communion, frequent worship, and the forming of the lines of religious thought and expression upon the very definite mould and model of the Prayer Book—all these are things that ought to enter, far more than they do, into the home life and training of our households.

In the same way it seems to me, that the clergy are at fault in not obeying the old English canon of the daily saying of the Offices for Morning and Evening Prayer, publicly if they may, and if not, privately ; that people ought to learn the duty and desirableness of framing their lives upon this theory, so that instead of now and then coming to church when they can, they should rather make the order of their lives turn toward the benediction of the day, opening and closing with the public worship of the House of God.

I am concerned, too, I confess, about our faithfulness in using the Book of Common Prayer. There has been a certain recognized license about many things, tolerated partly because of a perpetual expectation of some change—which it seems to me ought to stop now.

This Church has absolutely decided, for instance—much to my regret—not to take the English rendering of the *Te Deum*, in spite of the fact that certain favorite settings of music for that noble hymn seem to require the words "honorable" instead of "adorable", and "let Thy mercy lighten upon us." I think we ought to adapt whatever music we may use, to the American version of this hymn. And the "Thanks" after the Gospel, has been definitely decided against—also to my great regret—and ought, therefore, it seems to me, to be given up. The singing of the *Benedictus* before the Consecration in the Communion Office is plainly against the law of this Church, and, consequently, ought not to be done; and so I might go on. It is enough to say, that with the added liberty of use and the added richness of change, it becomes loyal and faithful priests to adhere to and abide by the final decisions of the highest authority that can speak to them upon this subject.

In this historic year, rich with venerable memories of the men who made the Book, and the Book that made the men, we may well make thankful recognition to Almighty God, of the grace and guidance of His Holy Spirit through the one hundred years and more of our ecclesiastical and liturgical growth. The Book of Common Prayer, not an utterance of our devotions merely, but the moulding power of our characters and lives, is the noblest possible expression of the religion of Jesus Christ. It stands beside the Holy Scriptures in the Authorized Version, resonant with the same stirring "English undefiled" that marks the vast superiority of the King James Bible over all other efforts at translation. It holds up before all men in its Creeds, its Catechism, and its sacramental Offices, the roundness and completeness of the Catholic Faith. It is almost like a great cathedral echoing with the songs of centuries. The old Psalter that made up the worship in which the Blessed Lord united with the Church of the older Dispensation; the hymn, perhaps at least, of Ambrose, which we call *Te Deum;* the inspired songs which broke from the full heart of the Blessed Mother of the Son of God and of the father of His forerunner; the prayers of the "golden-mouthed" bishop, and the thrice holy hymn of the angels—these make it almost true to say that it is a temple, richly decked with the carvings in stone, and the figures radiant with sunlight through the windows, of martyrs, and prophets, and apostles, and angels, and the saints of the holy Church throughout all the world. It finds its way, by frequent and familiar use, into the heart and conscience of the child; and as its "heavenly notes" fix their sweet harmonies upon the memory of childhood, they make the indelible impression of their truth upon the whole life afterwards. It is the password of that fellowship among English-speaking people, which makes us akin with all the wide-spread families of this great conquering race, and at home everywhere in the old fatherland across the sea, and in the new lands which own the sovereignty of England or the sweep of our American civilization. It is the silent preacher, the silent teacher—sent of God, as we believe—in the copies multiplied by millions through the restless energy of the press, thick as the leaves of Vallombrosa. It gathers and keeps all sacred memories of separate souls. It is the heritage and heirloom of an ancestry which carries us back to the upper room in Jerusalem, and to the underground churches where the dead slept, while the living sang hymns of victory over death. And it lifts us up and links us in with the worded glory, the articulate praise of the worship of the Paradise of God.

Surely, it is in the hearts and minds of all to thank God for the inestimable privilege of a share in the perfecting, possession, and preservation of that which so "procures reverence in the worship of God," and "promulgates the truths of the Gospel to mankind in the clearest, plainest, most affecting and majestic manner," to the glory of God through Jesus Christ our Lord.

# APPENDIX.

## Changes Incorporated into the Standard Prayer Book of 1892.

# APPENDIX.

## Changes Incorporated into the Standard Prayer Book of 1892.

### I. IN THE PRELIMINARY PORTION.

1. The Table of Contents has been made to conform to the actual contents. New Tables have been provided for finding Easter-day, the Dominical Letter, etc., with a Note as to the Ecclesiastical Full Moon.

2. Under the general title *Concerning the Service of the Church*, the following paragraphs have been prefixed to the *Order how the Psalter is appointed to be Read:*

"The Order for Morning Prayer, the Litany, and the Order for the Administration of the Lord's Supper or Holy Communion, are distinct Services, and may be used either separately or together; *Provided*, that no one of these Services be habitually disused.

"The Litany may be used either in place of the Prayers that follow the *Prayer for the President of the United States* in the Order for Morning Prayer, or in place of the Prayers that follow the *Collect for Aid against Perils* in the Order for Evening Prayer.

"On any day when Morning and Evening Prayer shall have been said or are to be said in Church, the Minister may, at any other Service for which no form is provided, use such devotions as he shall at his discretion select from this Book, subject to the direction of the Ordinary.

"For days of Fasting and Thanksgiving, appointed by the Civil or by the Ecclesiastical Authority, and for other special occasions for which no Service or Prayer hath been provided in this Book, the Bishop may set forth such Form or Forms as he shall think fit, in which case none other shall be used."

3. In the *Order how the Psalter is appointed to be read*, there have been inserted a *Table of Proper Psalms* to be used on certain days, sixteen in number, and a *Table of twenty Selections of Psalms* which may be used on days for which Proper Psalms are not provided.

4. The provision that the Minister may, under certain circumstances, appoint the Psalms to be used on special days of Fasting and Thanksgiving has been omitted; but it is still provided that he may, in his discretion, appoint the Lessons to be used on such days and also on occasions of Ecclesiastical Conventions and of Charitable Collections.

5. The following paragraph has been inserted with reference to *Hymns and Anthems:*

"Hymns set forth and allowed by the authority of this Church, and Anthems in the words of Holy Scripture or of the Book of Common Prayer, may be sung before and after any Office in this Book, and also before and after Sermons."

6. In the Table of Feasts, the title *the Apostle* has been added to the name of St. Barnabas, and *The Transfiguration of our Lord* JESUS CHRIST has been inserted. In the Calendar, the *Transfiguration* has been assigned to the sixth day of August, with proper lessons, and certain changes have in consequence been made in the Tables of Lessons.

## II. IN THE ORDER FOR DAILY MORNING PRAYER.

1. It has been provided by rubric that, on any day not a Sunday, instead of the General Exhortation, the Minister may say:

"Let us humbly confess our sins unto Almighty God."

And it has been further provided that, on any day not a Sunday, the Minister may end the Morning Prayer with the Collect for Grace and 2 *Cor.* xiii. 14.

2. It has been also provided by rubric that, on any day when the Holy Communion is immediately to follow, the Minister may, at his discretion, pass at once from the opening Sentences to the Lord's Prayer, first pronouncing, "The Lord be with you. *Answer.* And with thy spirit. *Minister.* Let us pray."

Slight changes have been made in the order of the opening Sentences; and special Sentences have been added for the Church seasons.

4. The *Gloria Patri* is printed after the rubric which provides for its use after the Psalms and Canticles; and the *Gloria in excelsis* is not printed here, but a rubric provides that it may be used at the end of the whole Portion of the Psalms or Selection from the Psalter, as heretofore.

5. The *Benedictus*, to be sung or said after the Second Lesson, has been inserted in full before the *Jubilate*, a space being left after the first four verses, with a Note, *That save on the Sundays in Advent the latter portion may be omitted.*

6. A change has been made in the rubric before the Apostles' Creed, so that it reads as follows:

¶ *"Then shall be said the Apostles' Creed by the Minister and the People, standing. And any Churches may, instead of the words, He descended into hell, use the words, He went into the place of departed spirits, which are considered as words of the same meaning in the Creed."*

7. In the Apostles' Creed the word *again* has been inserted in the latter part of the fifth article, so that it reads :

"The third day he rose again from the dead."

8. A change has been made in the rubric after the *Prayer for the President of the United States,* so that it reads as follows:

¶ *" The following Prayers shall be omitted here when the* LITANY *is said, and may be omitted when the Holy Communion is immediately to follow."*

9. In the Prayer for All Conditions of Men, after the words, *in mind, body, or estate,* there have been added in brackets the words, *especially those for whom our prayers are desired,* a note providing that this may be said when any desire the prayers of the Congregation.

10. In the General Thanksgiving, after the words, *and to all men,* there have been added in brackets the words, *particularly to those who desire now to offer up their praises and thanksgivings for thy late mercies vouchsafed unto them,* a note providing that this may be said when any desire to return thanks for mercies vouchsafed to them.

## III. IN THE ORDER FOR DAILY EVENING PRAYER.

1. It has been provided by rubric that, on days other than the Lord's Day, the Minister may, at his discre-

tion, pass at once from the opening Sentences to the Lord's Prayer.

2. It has been also provided by rubric that, on any day, instead of the General Exhortation, the Minister may say:

"Let us humbly confess our sins unto Almighty God."

3. The word *Amen* is printed at the end of the Declaration of Absolution, without any rubric; and the rubric before the Lord's Prayer ends with the words, *repeating it with him.*

4. Slight changes have been made in the order of the opening Sentences; and special Sentences have been added for the Church seasons.

5. The *Gloria in excelsis* is printed after a rubric which provides that it may be used at the end of the whole Portion or Selection of Psalms.

6. The hymn *Magnificat* has been inserted before the *Cantate Domino*, to be sung or said after the First Lesson.

7. The hymn *Nunc dimittis* has been inserted before the *Deus Misereatur*, to be sung or said after the Second Lesson.

8. The same change has been made in the rubric before the Apostles' Creed as in Morning Prayer; and the word *again* has been inserted in the Creed.

9. The following versicles and responses have been inserted between the response, *And grant us thy salvation*, and the versicle, *O God, make clean our hearts within us:*

"*Minister.* O Lord, save the State.

*Answer.* And mercifully hear us when we call upon thee.

*Minister.* Endue thy Ministers with righteousness.

150  APPENDIX.

*Answer.* And make thy chosen people joyful.
*Minister.* O Lord, save thy people.
*Answer.* And bless thine inheritance.
*Minister.* Give peace in our time, O Lord.
*Answer.* For it is thou, Lord, only, that makest us dwell in safety."

10. A new *Collect for Aid against Perils*, and *Prayer for those in Civil Authority* have been inserted, and also the following rubrics.

¶ *In places where it may be convenient, here followeth the Anthem.*

¶ *The Minister may here end the Evening Prayer with such Prayer, or Prayers, taken out of this Book, as he shall think fit.*

11. The Prayer for All Conditions of Men and the General Thanksgiving are printed with the bracketed clause and marginal note, as in Morning Prayer.

## IV. IN THE LITANY.

1. The following Suffrage has been inserted after that for Bishops, Priests, and Deacons:

"That it may please thee to send forth labourers into thy harvest;
  *We beseech thee to hear us, good Lord.*"

2. The General Thanksgiving has been printed as in Morning and Evening Prayer.

3. The words *Here endeth the Litany* have been omitted.

## V. IN THE PRAYERS AND THANKSGIVINGS UPON SEVERAL OCCASIONS.

1. It has been provided by rubrics that the special Prayers shall be used before, and the special Thanks-

givings shall be used after, the General Thanksgiving; or that, if the General Thanksgiving is not said, both the special Prayers and the special Thanksgivings shall be used before the final Prayer of Blessing or the Benediction.

2. The *Prayer to be used at Meetings of Convention*, with the following rubric, has been removed to a place immediately after the *Prayer for Congress;* and changes have been made in the Prayer and the rubric.

3. There has been inserted after the *Prayer to be used at the Meetings of Convention*, a Prayer for the Unity of God's People.

4. There has been inserted after the *Prayer for the Unity of God's People*, a Prayer for Missions.

5. There have been inserted after the *Prayers for those who are to be admitted to Holy Orders*, Prayers for Fruitful Seasons, to be used on Rogation-Sunday and the Rogation-days.

6. There has been inserted after the *Thanksgiving for a Recovery from Sickness*, a Thanksgiving for a Child's Recovery from Sickness.

## VI. A PENITENTIAL OFFICE.

A Penitential Office for Ash Wednesday has been inserted after the Prayers and Thanksgivings upon Several Occasions, containing the Psalm li. and the special Ash-Wednesday prayers.

## VII. IN THE COLLECTS, EPISTLES, AND GOSPELS.

1. The rubric prescribing that the Collect, Epistle, and Gospel for the Sunday shall serve all the week after, unless otherwise ordered, has been placed after the general title; and after it there has been inserted:

¶ *The Collect appointed for any Sunday or other Feast may be used at the Evening Service of the day before.*

2. The Collect, Epistle, and Gospel for Christmas-day are ordered to serve for any days which there may be between the Innocents' Day and the Sunday after Christmas ; and those for the Epiphany, for Ash-Wednesday, and for Ascension-day are ordered to serve for every day after unto the next Sunday, except upon Saints' Days.

3. After the Gospel for Christmas-day there have been inserted a new Collect, Epistle and Gospel, which may be used at the first Communion when there are two celebrations of the Communion on that day.

4. The Collects, Epistles, and Gospels for St. Stephen's Day, St. John the Evangelist's Day, and the Innocents' Day, are printed after the Gospel for Christmas-day.

5. The second rubric after the Collect for Ash-Wednesday, with all that follows before the Epistle, has been omitted.

6. The *Gloria Patri* is printed at the end of the Anthems appointed to be used on Easter-day instead of the *Venite.*

7. After the Gospel for Easter-day there have been inserted a new Collect, Epistle, and Gospel, which may be used at the first Communion when there are two celebrations of the Communion on that day.

8. The title *The Twenty-fifth Sunday after Trinity* has been changed to
"The Sunday next before Advent;"
and in place of the rubric after the Gospel there has been substituted:

¶ *If there be more than twenty-five Sundays after*

*Trinity, the service of some of those Sundays that were omitted after the Epiphany shall be taken in to supply so many as are here wanting. And if there be fewer than twenty-five Sundays, the overplus shall be omitted.*

9. After the Gospel for St. James's Day, the Collect, Epistle, and Gospel are inserted for

The Transfiguration of Christ.

## VIII. IN THE ORDER FOR THE ADMINISTRATION OF THE LORD'S SUPPER.

1. At the end of the second rubric, for the words, *as soon as conveniently may be*, have been substituted the words, *within fourteen days after, at the farthest.*

2. The doxology has been omitted from the Lord's Prayer at the beginning of the service, so that it ends thus:

"But deliver us from evil. Amen."

3. The words, *as followeth*, have been omitted from the rubric before the Ten Commandments, and the following rubric has been inserted:

*The Decalogue may be omitted, provided it be said once on each Sunday. But* Note, *That whenever it is omitted, the Minister shall say the* Summary of the Law, *beginning,* Hear what our Lord Jesus Christ saith.

4. After the Summary of the Law, the following has been inserted:

"*Here, if the Decalogue hath been omitted, shall be said,*

   Lord, have mercy upon us.
   *Christ, have mercy upon us.*
   Lord, have mercy upon us.
   ¶ *Then the Minister may say,*"

5. The rubrical direction as to the reading of the Gospel has been put in the form, *Then, the People all standing up, he shall read the Gospel, saying;* and the rubric before the *Gloria tibi* has been put in the form, *Here shall be said or sung.*

6. In place of the first rubric after the *Gloria tibi* has been substituted this rubric, followed by the CREED:

¶ *Then shall be said the Creed commonly called the* Nicene, *or else the* Apostles' Creed; *but the Creed may be omitted, if it hath been said immediately before in Morning Prayer;* Provided, *That the Nicene Creed shall be said on Christmas-day, Easter-day, Ascension-day, Whitsunday, and Trinity-Sunday.*

7. For the first Offertory Sentence, there has been inserted Acts xx. 35.

And there have been added to the Offertory Sentences: Exod. xxv. 2; Deut. xvi. 16, 17; I. Chron. xxix. 11; I. Chron. xxix. 14.

8. Permission has been given by rubric to use the Offertory Sentences on any other occasion of Public Worship when the alms of the people are to be received.

9. It has been provided by rubric that, when the Alms and Oblations are presented, there may be sung a Hymn, or an Offertory Anthem in the words of Holy Scripture or of the Book of Common Prayer, under the direction of the Minister.

10. The following note has been prefixed to the Exhortation beginning, "Dearly beloved in the Lord":

*But* Note, *That the Exhortation may be omitted if it hath been already said on one Lord's Day in that same month.*

11. After the Preface beginning, "It is very meet, right, and our bounden duty," the Triumphal Hymn with its rubrics reads as follows:

¶ *Here shall follow the* PROPER PREFACE, *according to the time, if there be any specially appointed; or else immediately shall be said or sung by the Priest,*

Therefore with Angels and Archangels, and with all the company of heaven, we laud and magnify thy glorious Name; evermore praising thee, and saying,

HOLY, HOLY, HOLY, Lord God of hosts, ¶ *Priest* Heaven and earth are full of thy glory: Glory *and* be to thee, O Lord Most High. Amen. *People.*

12. In the Prayer of Consecration, the Oblation and the Invocation are printed as distinct paragraphs.

13. In the Prayer of Consecration, instead of the words, "he may dwell in them, and they in him," there have been substituted "he may dwell in us, and we in him."

14. A change has been made in the first rubric after the Prayer of Consecration, so that it reads as follows:

¶ *Here may be sung a Hymn.*

15. The second rubric after the Prayer of Consecration has been amended by inserting the words:

"*And sufficient opportunity shall be given to those present to communicate.*"

16. In the next to the last rubric, at the end of the Office, the word *though* has been substituted for *if.*

17. The two Exhortations, giving warning of the Communion, are printed at the end of the Office.

## IX. IN THE MINISTRATION OF PUBLIC BAPTISM OF INFANTS.

1. An addition has been made to the rubric before the first Exhortation, so that it reads as follows:

¶ *If they answer,* No: *then shall the Minister proceed as followeth, the People all standing until the Lord's Prayer.*

2. A part of the first sentence of the rubric before the Gospel has been omitted.

## X. IN THE MINISTRATION OF PRIVATE BAPTISM OF INFANTS.

1. The first form of certification has been changed.
2. The second form of certification ends with the words "*doth witness to our comfort.*"

## XI. IN THE MINISTRATION OF BAPTISM TO SUCH AS ARE OF RIPER YEARS.

1. The third rubric has been omitted; and the following has been inserted at and after the end of the second rubric:

*And standing there, the Minister shall say,*
Hath this person been already baptized, or no?

¶ *If they answer,* No: *then shall the Minister (the People all standing until the Lord's Prayer) proceed as followeth.*

2. The Thanksgiving after the Lord's Prayer has been conformed to that in the Service for the Baptism of infants.
3. In the closing Exhortation, and in the second rubric at the end of the Service, slight verbal changes have been made, and to the rubric a clause has been added as follows:

¶ *And in case of great necessity, the Minister may begin with the questions addressed to the candidate, and end with the thanksgiving following the baptism.*

4. The following has been placed as an additional rubric at the end of the Service:

¶ *If there be reasonable doubt concerning the baptism of any person, such person may be baptized in the man-*

*ner herein appointed; saving that, at the immersion or the pouring of water, the Minister shall use this form of words:*

If thou art not already baptized, N., I baptize thee In the Name of the Father, and of the Son, and of the Holy Ghost. Amen.

5. For the words "*these Persons*" or "*the Persons*," wherever they occur in the prayers, and for the words "*these Persons*," where they occur the second time in the third of the rubrics at the end of the Service, there have been substituted the words "*these* thy *Servants.*"

## XII. IN THE CATECHISM.

The word "again" has been inserted in the Creed, as in Morning and Evening Prayer.

## XIII. IN THE ORDER OF CONFIRMATION.

1. The first rubric has been changed, so that it reads as follows:

¶ *Upon the day appointed, all that are to be then confirmed, being placed and standing in order before the Bishop, sitting in his chair near to the Holy Table, he, or some other Minister appointed by him, may read this Preface following; the People standing until the Lord's Prayer.*

2. The following has been inserted after the Preface:

¶ *Then the Minister shall present unto the Bishop those who are to be confirmed, and shall say,*

Reverend Father in God, I present unto you these children [*or* these persons] to receive the Laying on of Hands.

3. After the Preface and the Presentation of the Candidates, there has been inserted:

¶ *Then the Bishop, or some Minister appointed by him, may say,*

Hear the words of the Evangelist Saint *Luke,* in the eighth Chapter of the Book of the *Acts of the Apostles.* [Here follows Acts viii. 14–18.]

4. The following rubric has been inserted after the final Blessing:

¶ *The Minister shall not omit earnestly to move the Persons confirmed to come, without delay, to the Lord's Supper.*

## XIV. IN THE FORM OF SOLEMNIZATION OF MATRIMONY.

A clause has been inserted in the Exhortation, so that it reads as follows, after the words "holy Matrimony": "which is an honourable estate, instituted of God in the time of man's innocency, signifying unto us the mystical union that is betwixt Christ and his Church: which holy estate Christ adorned and beautified with his presence and first miracle that he wrought in Cana of Galilee, and"—

## XV. IN THE ORDER FOR THE VISITATION OF THE SICK.

The Commendatory Prayer has been changed by the omission of the last clause.

## XVI. IN THE COMMUNION OF THE SICK.

1. The following rubric has been inserted between the second and the third of the rubrics after the Gospel:

¶ *In the times of contagious sickness or disease, or when extreme weakness renders it expedient, the follow-*

*ing form shall suffice: The Confession and the Absolution;* Lift up your hearts, *etc., through the* Sanctus ; *The Prayer of Consecration, ending with these words,* partakers of his most blessed Body and Blood ; *The Communion; The Lord's Prayer; The Blessing.*

2. The following rubric has been added at the end :

¶ *This Office may be used with aged and bed-ridden persons, or such as are not able to attend the public Ministration in Church, substituting the Collect, Epistle, and Gospel for the Day, for those appointed above.*

## XVII. IN THE ORDER FOR THE BURIAL OF THE DEAD.

1. In place of the Rubric and Anthem after the Sentences, there has been substituted this rubric, after which are printed separately the parts of the former Anthem, each followed by the *Gloria Patri.*

¶ *After they are come into the Church, shall be said or sung one or both of the following Selections, taken from the* 39*th and* 90*th Psalms.*

2. The following rubric has been inserted immediately after the Lesson :

¶ *Here may be sung a Hymn or an Anthem; and, at the discretion of the Minister, the* CREED, *and such fitting* PRAYERS *as are elsewhere provided in this Book, may be added.*

3. The Lesser Litany has been inserted before the Lord's Prayer, with a new rubric, as follows :

¶ *Then the Minister shall say,*
Lord, have mercy upon us.
*Christ, have mercy upon us.*
Lord, have mercy upon us.

4. After "the grace of our Lord," etc., there have been inserted three additional Prayers.

5. The following rubric has been added :

¶ *Inasmuch as it may sometimes be expedient to say under shelter of the Church the whole or a part of the service appointed to be said at the Grave, the same is hereby allowed for weighty cause.*

6. At the end of the Office has been added the form to be used *At the Burial of the Dead at Sea,* slightly modified.

## XVIII. IN THE CHURCHING OF WOMEN.

A change has been made in the third rubric, so that it reads as follows :

¶ *Then shall be said by both of them the following* Hymn, *the woman still kneeling.*

## XIX. IN THE FORMS OF PRAYER TO BE USED AT SEA.

1. The title before the third Prayer has been changed so as to read, *Prayers to be used in all Ships in Storms at Sea.* The prayers that have reference to a storm and those that have reference to the enemy have been grouped separately ; and the Lord's Prayer has been placed immediately after the Absolution.

2. The forms belonging to Thanksgiving after a Storm and those belonging to Thanksgiving after a Victory have been arranged under distinct headings.

3. The form of Committal at the Burial of the Dead at Sea has been omitted here.

## XX. IN THE VISITATION OF PRISONERS.

1. The words *Minister* and *Answer* have been omitted before the Versicles ; and the Prayers have been placed

together after the *Miserere* (the printing of which is omitted), together with a new Prayer substituted for the Collect.

2. After the title, *A Form of Prayer for Persons under sentence of death*, the rubric reads:

¶ *When a criminal is under sentence of death, the Minister shall proceed to exhort him after this form, or other like.*

3. In place of the rubric after the Blessing the following rubric and notice are inserted:

¶ *At the time of Execution, the Minister shall use such devotions as he shall think proper.*

Notice. *It is judged best that the Criminal should not make any public profession or declaration.*

4. The *Prayer for Imprisoned Debtors* is omitted.

## XXI. IN A FORM OF PRAYER AND THANKSGIVING.

1. The Anthem has been conformed to the Prayer-Book version of the Psalter; there has been inserted, for the fourth verse of the Anthem, the seventh verse of Psalm cxlvii., and the *Gloria Patri* is printed at the end of the Anthem.

2. The special Thanksgiving has been changed to include an acknowledgment of the "blessings of Thy merciful providence bestowed upon this nation and people."

## XXII. IN THE PSALTER, ETC.

1. The 141st Psalm has been assigned to the evening instead of the morning of the twenty-ninth day of the month.

2. In place of the ten Selections of Psalms, the *Table*

of *Proper Psalms* and the *Table of Selections of Psalms* are inserted, as in the Order *Concerning the Service of the Church.*

3. The *Selections of Psalms for Holy Days*, which immediately precede the Psalter, have been omitted.

4. The numbers of the Psalms are printed in common numerals, and the verses of Psalm cxix. are numbered continuously.

5. The verses of the Canticles and the Psalms are in every case printed with the musical colon.

## XXIII. IN THE FORM AND MANNER OF MAKING, ORDAINING, AND CONSECRATING BISHOPS, PRIESTS, AND DEACONS.

1. In the Ordering of Priests and in the Consecration of Bishops, provision has been made for the saying of the Nicene Creed.

2. In the Consecration of Bishops, the longer paraphrase of the *Veni, Creator Spiritus*, has been omitted, and in place of the rubric *Or this*, there has been inserted:

¶ *Or else the longer paraphrase of the same Hymn, as in the Ordering of Priests.*

3. In the Litany and in the Order for the Administration of the Lord's Supper as printed in connection with the Ordinal, the same changes have been made as have been made in the same Services where they are printed elsewhere; except that, in the Order for the Administration of the Lord's Supper appended to the Ordinal, the word "Bishop" has been substituted for the word "Priest."

## XXIV. IN THE FORM OF CONSECRATION OF A CHURCH OR CHAPEL.

1. The rest of the former title has been omitted.
2. The *Gloria Patri* is printed at the end of Psalm 24.
3. A slight change has been made in the Prayers.
4. Alternative Lessons have been provided, as follows: First Lesson, Genesis 28 v. 10; Second Lesson, Revelation 21 v. 10.
5. In place of the four rubrics after the Gospel, a new one has been inserted.
6. In the last Prayer before the Benediction, the eleven words next following the words "the saints upon the earth," are omitted.

## XXV. IN AN OFFICE OF INSTITUTION OF MINISTERS INTO PARISHES OR CHURCHES.

1. The rest of the former title has been omitted.
2. A change has been made in the first rubric after the Letter of Institution, so that the part before the words, *the Wardens*, reads as follows:

¶ *On the day designated for the new Incumbent's Institution, at the usual hour of Morning Prayer, the Bishop, or the Institutor appointed by him, attended by the new Incumbent, and by the other Clergy present, shall enter the Chancel. Then all the Clergy present standing in the Chancel or Choir, except the Bishop, or the Priest who acts as Institutor, who shall go within the rails of the Altar;*

3. All reference to Institution by a Standing Committee, or to the Institution of an Assistant Minister, has been omitted.

4. The rubrics have been modified so as to provide for the Bishop as Institutor, though he may appoint a Priest to act for him in the Service, and the Letter of Institution may be read by another.

5. In the rubric before the form of delivery of the books, the word *State* has been changed to *Diocesan*.

6. The Anthem *Laudate Nomen* has been omitted; and it is provided that in its place Psalm lxviii. or Psalm xxvi. shall be said or sung.

### XXVI. THE ARTICLES OF RELIGION

are printed at the end of the book and have a distinct title-page.

---

### PREPARATION OF THE STANDARD BOOK OF 1892.

It was the duty of the committee appointed at the General Convention of 1889 " to prepare a Standard Prayer Book," to incorporate into the existing book the changes which had been finally adopted in 1886 and 1889, and to prepare for the incorporation of those which should be finally adopted in 1892. And it was also their duty to determine, as far as possible, what is the exact text of the Book of Common Prayer, to correct all typographical errors, and to make arrangements for printing the book in accurate form. The making of the additions and alterations, which had been constitutionally ordered by the General Convention in the process of the work of Liturgical Revision, was comparatively easy; but it was necessary to give much study to matters connected with the determination of the exact text of the Prayer Book, and the way in which it should be printed. The committee, in pursuing their work, had before them copies of the seven Standard editions of the American Book of Common Prayer, and of other editions of value for illustrating them; English books of various dates, and in particular the recently published fac-simile of the manuscript book appended to the Act of Uniformity of 1662; Scottish and Irish books, and copies of the English Bible dating from the first edition of the Great Bible, in 1539 (a superb copy of which was secured for their use), to the best modern editions of the so-called Authorized Version from the presses of the two Universities and of the Queen's Printers, with reprints of earlier versions. They had, of course, the advantage of much excellent work that had been done in the preparation of earlier Standards, and in particular were under obligations to the Standard of 1793, edited by Bishop White, and to that of 1845, edited with great and painstaking learning by the Rev. Dr. T. W. Coit. And they had at their disposal the results of much diligent labor which had been given for many years to Prayer Book study, and were specially indebted to the Rev. Frederick Gibson, the Rev. H. A. Metcalf, and the Rev. Dr. H. R. Percival for putting most valuable material at their disposal : while for accurate examination of tables and correction of final proofs they owed much to the Rev. Professor Barbour, of the Berkeley Divinity School.

In glancing briefly at the work of editing the new Standard, it will be well to speak separately of the passages of Holy Scripture other than the Psalter, the Psalter itself, and the remaining portions of the Book of Common Prayer.

I. The Epistles and Gospels in the Prayer Book, and part of the other passages from Scripture, are taken from the version of 1611, commonly known as the "Authorized Version." In the years which have elapsed since 1662, when the Epistles and Gospels in the English book were taken from this "last translation," the punctuation and orthography of this version have been greatly changed ; but the changes have been made by the responsible representatives of the King's Printers and of the two Universities, with the assistance of competent scholars. The first duty undertaken by the committee was to correct the Epistles and

Gospels by editions of this version which were certified by the authorized English publishers.

The Psalter, as will be stated presently, is in the translation which was made for the so-called "Great Bible" of 1539. From the Great Bible were also taken, but with some modifications, most of the Offertory Sentences, the verse from Job 14 : 1 in the Burial Office, and the prayer of blessing from 2 Cor. 13 : 14. The other passages of Holy Scripture contained in the Prayer Book, are the Ten Commandments, the Comfortable Words in the Communion Office, and the verse beginning "I heard a voice" in the Burial Office, together with the three New Testament Hymns (*Benedictus, Magnificat,* and *Nunc dimittis*) and the *Benedicite.* These were not taken from any version of the Bible, but were translated for the Services when they were compiled, probably by Archbishop Cranmer; only the original form of the last of the Comfortable Words was nearly that of the Great Bible. These four Words were inserted in the Order of Communion of 1548, in a form somewhat different from that which appears in the present English book; and in our book they have been further modified through the influence of Bishop Seabury's Communion Office.

II. The Psalter in the Prayer Book, as has

been said, was taken, at the time when the Services of the English Church were put into the vernacular or "vulgar tongue," from the Great Bible, the later editions of which are often known as Cranmer's Bible. It has been generally believed that the actual Prayer Book Psalter was taken from the fourth folio edition of this version; but the researches of the Rev. Frederick Gibson have shown that in reality it was from editions of a later date. There is, then, no present text of the Psalter, with modern spelling and punctuation, which stands in exactly the same position as the present text of the Authorized Version of the Bible. The committee followed the text of the Psalter in Dr. Coit's Standard of 1845, correcting it (when necessary) from the best available English Prayer Books, these in turn from the manuscript book of 1662, and this again from editions of the Great Bible itself.

III. The work upon the rest of the Prayer Book was largely done by reading the whole book, as if aloud, with the view of detecting inaccuracies or infelicities of punctuation; by comparing one part with another, in order to remove inconsistencies or lack of uniformity; and by the examination of all former Standards, or editions illustrating Standards, that the exact authorized text might be determined. It would not be possible, nor, if it were possible, would it be of interest to the reader, to undertake to mention at all in detail the results of the labor which was bestowed upon this part of the work. Most of them will never be seen except by the few who shall compare the new book with the old; but it is confidently believed that they will contribute much to the understanding and the intelligent use of the offices in the Book of Common Prayer.

This outline of the work of the committee in the Standard Book of Common Prayer may be closed with a quotation from their official report to the General Convention:

" Within the last forty-five years much study has been given to the English and the American Prayer Books, as to their origins, their history, their interpretation, and their text. We have felt that it would be a wrong to the Church if a report presented in this year should not show the results of this study, so far as it has been made available; and we have endeavored to present these wherever, under the principles already stated, they affect the determination of the proper form of our book."

THE END.

www.ingramcontent.com/pod-product-compliance
Lightning Source LLC
Chambersburg PA
CBHW032155160426
43197CB00008B/927